Pieces of My Heart

Pieces of
My Heart

Everyone has
an Everest

Jim Klobuchar

NODIN PRESS

ISBN 10: 1-932472-50-9
ISBN 13: 978-1-932472-50-9
Library of Congress Control Number: 2007932321
11   10   09   08   07   1   2   3   4   5   6

Design and layout: John Toren

Photo credits:

Rod Wilson 7-8, 98-99, 128, 131
Stormi Greener 9
Jim Klobuchar front cover, 46-47, 65, 92, 107,133,150, 153, 157
John Toren 12, 20, 23, 121, 140
Ed Solstad 25
Monte Later 53-54, 60, 61
Doug Kelley 57
Jerry Stebbins 78, 81, 83
Lloyd Luecke 108
Tom Porter 162
Jerome Carlson 175

The photo on the front cover shows Werner Burgener, climbing
partner of Jim Klobuchar, nearing the summit of the Eiger in
Switzerland.

Nodin Press is a division of Micawber's, Inc.
530 N. Third Street, Suite 120
Minneapolis, MN 55401

This is for my father, Mike,
an iron miner who opened the world for me.
He flew just once, over the woods and lakes
he revered. We were together, flying
into the late afternoon sun.
It was the most precious hour of all.

Acknowledgements

The author wishes to thank the *Minneapolis Star Tribune*, Voyageur Press of St. Paul, MN, Kirk House Publishing of Edina, MN, and Ralph Turtinen Publishing Co. for permission to reprint portions of his writings that originally appeared in their publications.

Special gratitude is expressed to the Knopf Publishing division of Random House for the inclusion of excepts from the writings of Sigurd Olson, which appear in Chapters 15 and 21 of this book, and appeared originally in *Reflections from the North Country* and *Wilderness Days* published by Alfred A. Knopf; and to photographer Craig Blacklock and Blacklock Nature Photography of Moose Lake, MN, for permission to reprint a quotation from Sigurd Olson that appeared originally in *The Hidden Forest*, a collaboration between Mr. Olson and Les Blacklock, Craig Blacklock"s father.

The author also wishes to thank Charles Dayton for gathering a collection of Sigurd Olson's reflections published during Mr. Olson's long and distinguished career of advocacy in the cause of conservation and in his lyrical writings on the gifts of wild nature. Thanks also are due to Larry Gates of Portal, AZ, for permission to reprint excerpts from reflections on natural mysticism gathered on his website, and Joan Larsen of Park Forest IL for her thoughts and experiences in that fascinating genre. Our thanks also are extended to Rod Wilson of Eden Prairie, MN, Jerry Stebbins of the Twin Cities, Tom Porter of Beaver Bay, MN, Monte Later of St. Anthony, ID, Sarah Levar of the Dorothy Molter Museum in Ely, MN, and Northland College of Ashland, WI, for permission to print original photographs they made available to us. Thanks also to the *Minneapolis Star and Tribune* photo department and Peter Coleman for permission to reprint a photo of Jim and Amy Klobuchar preparing for their cross country bike ride.

The author expresses special gratitude to Joan Larsen for her passionate remembrances and depiction of days "that will last forever" in Patagonia and in the Antarctic; for her exploration of the belief that there is an actual heaven on earth, and for suggesting the title of this book.

The author also extends professional thanks and admiration for the skilled and valuable editing of John Toren, and the courtesies and advice of Norton Stillman of Nodin Press, the publisher of this book.

Finally, the author expresses loving thanks to his daughters, Amy and Meagan, for tolerating his single-minded conviction that it was possible to hike from Meiringen to the Grosse Scheidegg in a snowstorm in the Swiss Alps without colliding with a resident flock of baffled sheep. It wasn't, but it WAS suspenseful.

Contents

Preface

When we walk in the woods on a weekend we often do it with a kind of light-hearted reverence. We feel a comfort and an intimacy with the woods, the bird calls and shafts of sunlight bent by the density of the forest. We might also experience those feelings while walking an uninhabited seashore, in tune with the sounds and rhythms of the surf. It heaves and recedes, timeless and enigmatic, as though it carries the secrets of the ages. And it's not going to give us the answers.

Fair enough. We've received more than we gave. When we leave to resume the usual workaday hustle and turmoil, we KNOW something good has entered our lives or been restored to them. Early in this book I ask a question: What is it that touched us with peace?

The widely admired naturalist, Sigurd Olson, believed this: each of us is a kind of incarnation of what has preceded us on earth from its very beginnings, reflected in our longings and ambitions, in our capacity to create and find beauty, and in our search for identity. That search, he believed, flows from a fundamental need to re-connect with the nature that gave us life and now in some form still nurtures us.

This may be a poetic view of the strivings and needs of human beings. But who's to say that it doesn't come close to a core truth? We are fascinated by the fireplace. It, too, expresses something that comforts us. Ages ago fire kept human beings alive. Do those primitive, life-or-death recognitions of fire, through thousands of years in the genetic stream, translate today to our fondness for a campfire?

This book is about one man's discoveries in a lifetime's experience in wild nature. It was not my highest priority. Apart from personal relationships, making a living in daily newspapering probably ranked higher. But with reasonable ingenuity I managed to combine work with roaming. What impelled me into the woods and mountains is not as important to me as what I drew from them. And what I drew from them 30 and 40 years ago was not what I found later.

The relationships changed. Where I felt certain moments of triumph and exhilaration years ago—in challenging nature, extracting thrills, reaching the summits—the rewards later changed into something quieter. The gifts I identify now became the more durable ones. They brought into my life some extraordinary people whose uniqueness became a kind of mentorship for me: Dorothy Molter, who lived alone on an island, at peace with the woods and animals and at ease with herself; Eddie Pizzarro, a Peruvian guide and a generous viewer of the human condition, the Sherpas of the Himalayas, the Lhakpas and the Gyaltsens, the villagers, the poor who did not seem demeaned by what they lacked but invited us into their lives and their homes.

The gifts have included a deeper appreciation of our relationships with the earth where we travel; the mountains, the Nile, the great sweep and silence of the Serengeti savannah at night, the loneliness of Minnesota's northwoods in winter, the mischief of the Yellowstone's hot springs; the memories of a beautiful man of the Teton Mountains, Glenn Exum and the undefeatable Linda Phillips, disabled all of her adult life, energized by both the storms of the north country and its aurora borealis. She was as lovely, as frail and yet as tough as the lady slippers in the woods where her ashes now lie.

But the gifts have also included the impromptu wackiness that came with some of those encounters—battling a larcenous Canada Jay in the winter Boundary Waters, and mounting some homespun strategy against encroaching lions in Africa.

And with all of this has come a thanksgiving. To whom or what? My grandmother immigrated from Slovenia and like most immigrants brought with her the culture and superstitions of what they called the "old country." When she was a little girl, and thunder and lighting shook the sky, her parents cheerfully seized on all of these percussions as a teaching opportunity.

God was angry, they said. He was angry because people were misbehaving. And these people, she was reminded pointedly, included Little Girls.

"So Don't Misbehave!"

I doubt that my grandmother bought into that particular catechism. This didn't make her shy about trying to inflict it on her grandchildren, including me. Grandma was full of fun and surprises and ultimately I caught on to her little tricks. But she did get my attention. In a comical way it was my introduction to an idea that many people take very seriously, and with reason: the relationship between the earth on which we live, what we call nature, and Something Higher.

This book touches only sparingly on what that relationship is or might be. I leave that turf largely to the theologians. But the subject is too inviting and juicy to avoid. Anybody can jump in, so I do.

The nature I've experienced has often brought me peace, wonderment and sometimes gratification when I have engaged its strength. It is a nature that can also be humbling, destructive, beautiful and vulnerable. It is our earth, and it is a pretty marvelous one. It is our nourishment and it badly needs our guardianship. For the adventurer, I've learned that the best road is not necessarily the road that takes us to the heights or to the most distant valleys or deepest woods.

The greatest virtue of the wild country in its personal impact is its power to deepen us has human beings. For some it has created goals of achievement, let's say a mountain summit. The subtitle of this book, Everyone Has an Everest, recognizes the human urge or need to reach an ultimate fulfillment. But it also recognizes that the Everests of our lives take widely diverse forms. There are less dramatic but more significant Everests—a college degree, attainment of our highest professional goals, overcoming illness, and more. Achieving peace in our lives is one of them.

And sometimes that peace begins with a discovery we make of ourselves in the midst of a nature that can be either wild or placid. Whether we are drawn to its power to excite us or its gift of healing, we may find that it has brought something different and enduring into our lives.

So the trail is open, and there's room for two.

– Jim Klobuchar, June 2007

1

The Dicey Search
for Shangri La

When I was a boy watching the movies I was introduced to the warm and fuzzy notion of a Shangri La, an idyllic valley said to be high in the Himalayas, isolated from the rest of the world. It was a place where people lived in unbroken serenity and were forever young. This hard-to-resist gem of latter-day mythology was incarnated by the novelist James Hilton in *Lost Horizon* and popularized in a film of the same name.

As an adolescent harkening to the first murmurings of romantic love, I was wafted into the possibilities of that remote and enchanted domain by the lyrics of a Top 40 tune:

Your kisses take me...to Shangri La.

Without blaming the minimal voltage power of those early kisses, I have to say they never quite launched me to Shangri La. But years later, with friends, I climbed a mountain called Pacharmo in the Nepalese Himalayas on the approaches to Tibet. It was snowing hard when we reached the Teshi Lapcha Pass, where we camped in a cave just below 20,000 feet the night before the climb. It was a wild and percussive bedlam of a night, filled with lightning bolts and the sounds of avalanches booming high above the ice cliffs. But in the sunlight after we returned from the mountain the next day, I walked for some distance over the pass and looked deep into what I could see of the Rolwaling Valley.

It was hidden, remote, and walled by rock precipices thousands of feet high. The clouds floating beneath the rock outcrop where I stood gave the valley and its neighboring ravines an other-worldly glory, deepened by the fir forests that climbed the mountain slopes and the snowfields that framed it. But it wasn't a time to linger. The Teshi Lapcha was icy and not easy, either up or down. And this was one horizon that wasn't lost, although it WAS four miles high.

And for just a moment I had a thought: If there ever was a Shangri La, this could pass as its epilogue.

But we know there is and was no Shangri La.

Don't we?

Still, there is a quirk in the human condition, the contrarian streak, that makes it hard for some to shake loose from a transforming idea: the need to take what Everester Lute Jerstad called "One Step Beyond." It nudges us to follow an elusive chalice forged by imagination, dream, ambition, wish, or faith: Utopia. Nirvana. Shangri La and, of course, Heaven. It is a quality that often propels us into serious exploration—the moon and the stars, for example, distant life in the galaxies. But just as often it provokes flights of whimsy when we start chasing the insoluble secrets of the universe and life.

One of the most engaging story tellers I've ever heard, the late Jay Beecroft of Minneapolis, was an armchair mountaineer when he wasn't traveling the world as a motivational speaker and the head of training for the 3M Company.

He was a friend of mine who was fascinated and marginally baffled by the exertions and the creeds of mountain climbing, or what he construed to be its creeds. We talked about it often during our travels together in the Swiss Alps and the Grand Tetons of Wyoming. He asked me what drives people to climb a mountain or to bicycle interminably up hills and down, in the rain and wind. And what moved *me* to do it?

I interrupted once to say tartly: "That's not a question, Beecroft. It's an accusation."

He was a whimsical guy. He didn't immediately deny it, but he clearly was curious about what he called all that striving and grunting and overcoming. Or, as the climber rose higher and higher was there something of the spiritual in it?

I nodded. "For some, yes."

Beecroft played football in college but he'd gained weight by middle age when I knew him and he had no pretensions about reaching some icy summit in the Karakoram. He hiked occasionally when we went into the mountains with Monte Later, a mutual friend from Idaho, and he thoroughly enjoyed those ramblings, especially when they were rewarded afterward with a temperate brandy and quality cuisine.

But Jay Beecroft liked to probe the whys of climbing. What *was* the allure of wild country, he asked, that it could provoke a presumably normal person to march off alone into the winter wilderness of northern Minnesota with a pair of skis and a sleeping bag, to camp at night to a baying chorus of hungry wolves.

I told him that as long as the wolves kept howling I never worried about it. "It's when I can't hear them that I get edgy."

"I don't think you're nuts," Jay said amicably. "In some ways I envy you."

I thanked him for his civility and he said, "you have to tell me that there is something more than bravado in this, something more than getting to the top or just doing it and getting out alive."

I said I thought I could make that case, but I wondered why he was doing a laboratory study on the human id in the middle of a perfectly harmless round of golf.

He thought this was fair question. "I talk in a lot of places," he said. "I enjoy it. The urges and the needs of human nature are part of that. I want to know what comes with all of the sweat and what results from the risk."

I took the bait cordially. "You mean like finding the ever-mythical Shangri La."

He could have laughed at that but he didn't, because my reference to Shangri La had struck a bell. That was essentially where he was trying to go with his interrogation without delving too deeply into the murky water of psychoanalysis. Jay's mind was a broad and changing canvas. His interests and curiosities spread from the theater to serious literature, athletics, music, and particularly to the keys to human motivation. He spoke frequently to business groups, some of them accustomed to hearing high-velocity oratory from speakers who shook the decibel gauges, exhorting their corporate audiences to set the bar higher, exploit their strengths, carve a niche, et al. Jay was different. He often charmed listeners with his easy sophistication and drolleries. But he also offered sound menus for success and usually left his listeners feeling good about themselves, and their goal-oriented fervors, which could so easily get skewed and ramped from healthy ambition into self-defeating obsession.

Which may be why he liked telling the story of the rich man who gave away all of his wealth to devote the final years of his life to discovering the meaning of life. I loved hearing this tale because it had some fun with our often ponderous attempts to explain the eternal mysteries.

The rich man was worth hundreds of millions of dollars. He was past his prime but still healthy and very inquisitive about the grand design of life. He was, in fact, haunted by it. He sat down with his accountants and lawyers, set up all of his relatives for life, gave most of his remaining fortune to charities and then shipped out on a freighter bound for India. There he debarked with nothing but the clothes on his back and enough coin to keep him in food until, having crossed the border into Nepal, he reached the foothills of the great Himalaya.

The natives confirmed the information he had received in the lowlands. The rarest of wise men, they said, lived in contemplation more than ten thousand feet higher, above the cliffs and the fir forests where the great lammergeyer eagles soared. If there was any living person who could give him the answers to the mysteries of life this was the one.

For weeks the ex-tycoon, now a pilgrim, lived off the land, eating berries and wild greens, gaining altitude, fording icy rivers in the fearsome ravine of Lahoozrahad. He lost weight and slept in the open as night temperatures fell, covering himself with pine branches against the cold. He did this day after day until, nearly exhausted and reduced to skin and bone, he came to the promised little monastery in the highest reaches of the Himalaya, and asked to be shown to the prophet he had come thousands of miles to see.

The wise man welcomed him into his small study, smiling genially from a simple woven chair. Above him were shelves of worn red leather holy books containing the wisdom of the centuries. Breathing heavily and barely able to summon the energy in his state of exhaustion, the pilgrim spoke. "Oh, wise man," he said, "I have come thousands of miles and made great sacrifices to meet you. Tell me, Learned One, what is the meaning of life."

The wise man's kind face was the image of serenity and compassion. He placed his hands on the cheeks of the weary pilgrim and said:

"Life, my son, is a fountain."

The pilgrim looked slowly into the wise man's eyes. He sat in silence for a few moments. And then the pilgrim's eyes grew larger, his demeanor changed and his lips quivered. He stared fiercely into the eyes of the wise man and said:

"I have given away all of my fortune. I have come ten thousand miles. I have risked death and dragged my body through the fearsome Valley of Lahoozhrahad, escaped hyenas and crocodiles and forded icy rivers. My body is shrunken to the bone and I am within whispers of death. And I have finally asked you, oh wise man, what is the secret of life."

The pilgrim's eyes stayed fixed on the wise man, glowing astonishment and disbelief.

"And after all this, you tell me Life is a Fountain!"

The pilgrim rose, his face a mask of desolation and anger. "IS THAT ALL YOU HAVE TO SAY?"

The wise man sat motionless in the face of this indictment, staring at the pilgrim. Where before he was serene and self-possessed, the wise man now looked shattered and bewildered.

"You mean," he said finally, "life AIN'T a fountain?"

I have to tell you in all humility that I have visited monasteries not unlike the bereaved wise man's. I have seen those dusty prayer books and heard the blaring monotone horns that are part of the Buddhist and Hindu observances. I have smelled the incense, and on other days breathed the sweet scent of the burning juniper branches lit by the women harvesting potatoes. I've heard the drum beats and drum rolls signifying death in the Sherpa villages. I've climbed in the Himalaya and trekked in those mountains for more than 25 years and slept beneath rhododendron trees 30 feet high with red blossoms as big as balloons.

I can't say that I ever asked one of the monks for the meaning of life. Perhaps I was afraid that he would dismiss me as some crank cribbing material for a reality show.

He may, though, have been able to tell us something more valuable.

Something about the tranquility and good will available to us if we

allow these to be liberated from our tensions and fears.

Easily said. But this is what you will often feel when you walk in the rhododendron forests in the Himalaya.

I've placed my recollections of Jay Beecroft at the beginning of this book because of his good-natured spoofing of some of the clichés of search and adventure. Yet Jay could never quite conceal the fact that his own life had its quests, and mysticism might even have crept into the edges of it. The questions Jay asked are pertinent still. When we talked 25 and 30 years ago I was in the midst of breakneck agendas of work, writing, speaking, roaming, climbing, flying, cycling, skiing, parachuting. Life was a rampage of action. Some of it affected my personal relationships. Some of it forced me to back up and to recognize that the truly great gifts of wild nature *were* more spiritual than visceral, and that a climb in the mountains or a day of skiing in the woods was more a time of discovery than a mark of achievement. Nature as sanctuary rather than arena.

It did take those values and discoveries a long time to surface.

But unless you are completely numb you eventually come to understand the restorative powers of the rushing wind, orchestrating a concert of sound in a pine forest. Or the silences of the night as you lie in your sleeping bag waiting for the first tints of sunlight and the last two thousand feet to the summit.

Such an interlude can become so intimate and cleansing, and the union with nature so powerful, that you become convinced there is a divinity in it.

After all of these years, all these adventures, I have no quarrel with that belief.

I don't worship nature as God. My theology has trouble enough reconciling the behavior of human beings with the beliefs we profess and the scriptures and canons we nimbly ignore.

But I know there is something more than the might of granite and moving ice on Dhaulagiri and the Annapurna Range of the Himalayas. In the late afternoon's dim and refracted light you can walk through the forest of sycamores and hanging moss below the Gorapani Pass, where the wind and the swaying trees create sounds—secret moans and creakings. In my childhood I would have taken these to be the sounds of a witch's forest. But in the Himalaya it is not a wicked queen but Annapurna who rules. Annapurna the goddess of nurture and the harvest.

(Next page) Thousands of Himalayan climbers and trekkers have passed Ama Dablam on their way to the approaches to Everest. Some call it a perfect mountain. Why would anyone argue?

It is not the mysterious sounds that I remember best from that forest, however. It's a Sherpa guide named Ang Nima. As a young guide he had refused to leave the bodies of four trekkers struck by an avalanche. He stayed through the freezing night, praying his mantras, keeping his vigil, faithful to his commitment.

A quiet little man, now in his forties, Ang Nima was walking the trail with us, responding quickly when we needed something, making himself useful. He was a mountaineer who never felt he lessened his self-respect by doing the menial chores required of a trekking Sherpa. He smiled often but rarely spoke because the English language was basically a mystery to him in those years. And then as we neared camp, close to a village where he lived, Ang Nima disappeared into the forest and emerged a few minutes later, his brown face lit by a smile. In his hand he held three wild orchids and gave one to each of the three women in our party.

It was a bouquet, a gift of the forest that said, "this is from my house to you."

One of the women wept.

I listen with some respect to people who have traveled the wild country often and who don't have the flimsiest concept of the hereafter. But they will tell me this without compromise or doubt: that the one time they are likely to experience an indescribable moment of peace and fulfillment here on earth—something close to the rapture or Nirvana promised by prophets, serious and otherwise—is when they stand in the waning rays of the sun above a deep gorge in Africa or Nepal, or above the Sacred Valley of the Urubamba in Peru.

Why would you argue?

It's a belief. An affirmation. The moment is divine if you believe it is divine.

That is the kind of power and beauty that experiencing wild nature can hold. Perhaps I'm less gifted, or less astute, than those who discover a heaven on earth, and I admit not having the foggiest idea of the possibilities available to us, good and bad, when we leave this life. A minister friend of mine said, "I don't know, either. All I know is that God more or less has taken care of me here on earth and I have to believe it will be the same hereafter."

It is a homely but workable hypothesis. It leaves me room to explain the extraordinary moments I have felt in a lifetime of search and discovery. That includes the effects on my life of chance encounters with people who deepened it, and places and events and scenes that have cleansed some of my self-indulgences.

These I simply call the grace in my life.

My spiritual mentors tell me that grace, if it's the grace of God we're talking about, does not have to be deserved.

That is a comfort.

But it seems to me that finding grace doesn't have to be left to chance, either. The definition of grace, of God or whatever moves in our lives that is supernatural, is not going to be settled here.

I do know that when we open our minds and our spirits to the nourishing power of wild nature and to the discoveries it brings into our lives, the results are not only enriching. Sometimes they are amazing. We change. We find new roads. New people come into our lives. Getting older is suddenly not as onerous. Life may not be a fountain. But it can be an unexpected burst of sunlight and fresh air.

Wise men in the mountains of Asia may not be meteorologists, but they do know something about the environment. When we discover a way to live in harmony with it, to draw both excitement and repose from it, we probably have come a little closer to the fountain.

2

Nature Violent, Nature Benign:

A Fatherless Indian Boy Finds His Legacy

You hear the avalanche before you see it. The sound is deep-throated and irreversible. Everything human within range stops in its tracks. It is a fearsome prelude to a violent and terrible act of nature that will disgorge millions of tons of snow and ice within seconds down the mountain slope. But for a moment there is no movement on the snow slope. For a climber or skier who is caught in the path of the ensuing cascade, with no time to escape, that first muffled crunch when the snow pack tears free is the crack of doom.

On another day, though, when an avalanche high in the mountains presents no threat to life, it can be a sight of astonishing beauty.

Here was a day in the Himalayas. The trekkers moved slowly on the flanks of the Khumbu Glacier a few miles from Everest itself, when we heard that distinctive crump and rending high up on the Nuptse Face, which is a contiguous part of the Everest massif. The sound wasn't a thunder and it wasn't particularly terrifying because it was at least three miles away, on the far side of the glacial moraine where we were hiking. Seconds later the white cataract came racing down the cliffs, thousands of feet, gaining speed, a thick cloud of snowdust forming above it.

We stopped and stood motionless. The avalanche was booming as it descended; and then the megatons of snow struck the floor of the glacial ravine with enormous energy and a gale of snowdust blew across the glacier toward us.

Where we stood more than a mile away we had nothing to fear. The avalanche had largely spent its force. The snow cloud sped rapidly towards us but was little more than a breeze when it reached us. For two or three minutes we were wrapped in a kind of harmless whiteout, ice chips and snow flecking our faces. But it was a part of wild nature few of us had experienced—a rampaging nature of immense power, seemingly alien, a power that might have been deadly on another day yet somehow seemed a gift to us on that day.

And why? It was a gift for me because for those few minutes we experienced a force that seemed almost unearthly in its strength. Yet in the moments when we were enveloped by the benign snow cloud we seemed spiritually fused to this phenomenon and absorbed in it.

For me it brought even closer a paradox of wild nature that has fascinated and aroused me whenever I've encountered it. The paradox is that the same force can on one day be good and healing and even sublime influence in the lives of millions, and on the next become a homicidal hurricane or a tidal wave.

Does the God who created the one also create the other? Or in the poetic figure of William Blake, "Did He who made the lamb make thee?" (the tiger burning bright).

If there is divinity in the peace we feel and the sanctuaries we seek in the woods and lake country—and how many among us will deny those convictions—then how do we come to grips with the catastrophic behavior this same "divine" nature sometimes exhibits?

Where is the God in all of this?

The question seems reasonable enough to me. As an act of mercy to my friends and relatives, I make no claim to being a theologian. I have a basic belief that there is someone, something beyond our understanding and conception, that gave rise to the creation of the earth in which we live, and also to our humanity. And that nature both nourishes us and sometimes hurts us because we are not wise enough to know when or how to manage it or to integrate it with our lives. In a book I wrote a few years, I visualized a 60-minute conversation with God. To make it happen God generously arrived for the interview in corporeal form—jeans and turtle neck as I remember. No gray beard was in sight. While the introductions went well, I thought, I was intimidated by the unwritten protocol of this kind of meeting. I asked for help. "How should I address you," I asked.

"How about 'God,' he said. 'That's nice and unambiguous'"

The talk got around to a point raised by the respected rabbi, Harold Kushner, who asked how we should react when bad things happen to good people. The talk with God eventually segued to my thoughts about nature and natural disasters. My response was a theology which might or might not survive the seminaries. It asked for a kind of one-size-fits-all logic that would leave room for both a creative, benevolent force and the random destructive behavior of both humanity and nature.

My solution to this evident paradox was something like this:

"God created nature and the laws of nature," I said, "and then let nature be nature.

"God gives human beings a will of their own, the knowledge of what's right and what's wrong, which we often call conscience, and then he let's human beings be human beings."

I'm not sure of the final grade in all of this, and I assume it will be available somewhere in the future. Mine is one life that has been seasoned by wild nature in ways that in my mid- years made me blush. They have ranged from red meat thrill-seeking to the rediscovery of a spirituality. I didn't foresee spirituality in my first struggles on mountain walls, with adventures of flight, parachuting, marathon runs, solo bike rides and scuba diving under three feet of ice on Lake Minnetonka.

In short, this is not necessarily a resume of a man in search of Shangri La.

I'm not sure when the transition came. Out of those early daredevil spasms I slowly moved into a genuine involvement with a nature I came to idealize, one in which I eventually found a grace that I couldn't possibly have identified earlier.

It might have begun when I met a teen-age Native American kid who had been invited into the Big Brothers program. I was a volunteer in the program and the boy, Jimmy, was an Ojibway. Jimmy's people had traditionally revered the northwoods. They were nurtured and sheltered by its land, water, and sun, and they prayed to a Great Spirit who bestowed it all.

And yet this 14-year-old boy from a broken family had never been north of Minneapolis and St. Paul. Apart from what he saw on television. He had no personal knowledge of the great stands of Norway and white pine to the north or the jeweled mornings of sunrise in the Boundary

Waters canoe country stretching from Ely to the north shore of Lake Superior. He had never seen the vast sweep of water his ancestors called Gitchi Gummi, the big sea water of Longfellow, Lake Superior. He didn't quite understand the relationship of the North Star, Polaris, to direction finding. He was unaware of the aurora borealis in performance, when it seems alive with its shifting streamers of green and yellow, pouring its mysterious light over the northland.

He wasn't a dynamic kid by nature. We both understood that a feeling-out process was necessary in these things. He was a kid who was alert and interested, a little cautious but also inquisitive.

He had never camped under stars, but he seemed ready. He had large round eyes and a head of brown hair that spread over his forehead in bangs and was usually left bare to the rain or sun. He confessed that he was a better fisherman than a basketball player, an admission with which I didn't quarrel after watching him go O for 10 throwing the basketball at the backboard on the outdoor court where we met. I made my own confession. It was part of the ice-breaking ritual. "As a fisherman," I said, "I couldn't get a bite in an aquarium. I don't have a rod. Maybe you can show me some techniques. We may not find many fish, but I think you may see something you haven't expected. We're going to see an ocean, right here in the middle of the country."

I described Lake Superior and handed Jimmy a map. He was the designated expedition navigator in charge of road signs and junctions. In less than three hours we had reached the cascades of the St. Louis River in Jay Cooke State Park and crossed the Interstate Bridge between Duluth and Superior, Wisconsin. Although it was late May, the ice pack of Lake Superior glistened to the northeast, as though signaling our arrival on another planet. Duluth weather has a deserved reputation for the bizarre, but this one came right out of the almanacs of make-believe. The temperature to the west was 85 degrees. In Duluth, refrigerated by an ice field stretching 10 miles across, it was 25 degrees cooler. Imagine waking up to find an iceberg in the middle of your front yard. But the water opened beyond Two Harbors 25 miles up the lake shore and the sun touched the pale blue surface with streaks of silver.

And now something happened almost as odd as the upside-down temperature readings. Cautious and quiet Jimmy was jabbering like a jay, describing the freighter five miles out in the lake, twisting around to watch the gulls overhead and then staring down at the swell rolling against the shoreline.

"You're right," he exclaimed. "It IS an ocean."

The irresistible place names declared the history and a little bit of the poetry of the North Shore of Lake Superior as we rode: Castle Danger, Split Rock Lighthouse, Gooseberry Falls, Baptism River, Father Baraga's Cross. We detoured six miles up the old Toonerville highway from Ilgen City toward Ely, just to see Lake Superior from high on the headland above its spreading size. And then we drove up the Sawbill Trail and found a place deep in the woods with a small opening in the trees. Through it we could see the dancing river below. We put up our orange and green tent and I went for water. When I got back the kid had built a fireplace of boulders, dragged in enough firewood for a three-week retreat and seemed poised to light a match.

We discussed that. I said I thought a fire was one option, but since it was 4 p.m., some trail time before supper was another. He agreed, and went looking for trails. A road sign led us to the trail to Eagle Mountain, and we hiked to the top of Minnesota's highest hill. Jimmy walked with energy and widening eyes. He used a makeshift walking stick that he kept breaking and replacing. Several times I heard him running to catch up, and I found out why when I stopped at a bend in the trail. He would stop to listen to a woodpecker or to examine the dead leaves of the forest humus. They weren't new to him. But their place in the forest, and *his* place in the forest, might have aroused new thoughts and questions in the mind of a fatherless kid who had never walked in the northwoods. At the top of Eagle Mountain a marker announced that we were at 2,301 feet. Jimmy flopped on the handiest flat rock. But after a few minutes he stood and walked a few feet to glimpse the distant wilderness lakes sunk deep in the twilight.

He looked up and seemed to be working out his thoughts.

"What are you thinking?" I asked.

"I think it's great," he said.

"So do I."

We ate stew and meat loaf cooked on our small camp stove. And then we sat by the campfire and talked about what he was going to be, a carpenter, a farmer or maybe a painter. He said he liked drawing pictures and he would draw some of the North Shore scenes when he got back to school. Before we got into our sleeping bags, the moon eased out of the clouds and rode above the noisy white water of the Temperance River and we watched its progress. The fire was still crackling. The woods were full of sound from the river, the fire and the insects. The night was alive and amiable, and it was a good time for conversation. We talked about little things. I asked what he had done with his last walking stick.

"I left it against a tree on the end of the trail," he said, "case somebody needs it."

I doubt that the northwoods taught Jimmy that simple courtesy. It was something he brought TO the woods, and it was a lovely gift. I wanted to confide in him at that moment. I wanted him to see how much joy I took having some small part in uniting this Native American boy with the wild country where his ancestors hunted and lived, and revered the land.

But that was grown-up kind of talk, I thought, and maybe I could tell him later in his life, when it might mean more.

I was wrong to withhold that thought, I know now.

The next morning when I left at sunrise to walk to the river, he was balled up in his sleeping bag. Only a trace of early-morning dampness touched the bushes and young leaves of the birches. It hadn't rained lately. There was a smell of dust in the air, but it was overmatched by the musky sweetness of the humus and the smell of the spring-cleansed pines. I walked to the edge of the river. It was noisy and fast, sluicing around the boulders which were its natural defenses against intruding canoers. The sun was doing its morning dance on the river but nothing moved in the forest except for the leaf of an overhanging hazel bush. It got splashed now and then by the tiny geysers of water thrown up where the river scurried into the rocks near shore.

One other thing moved. Jimmy was at my elbow, carrying a fishing rod and big expectations.

"Do you think I could catch a trout in this river?"

"I'll put it this way," I said. "Do you want me to hold breakfast until you catch a trout or should I set up Plan B the way they do in the Pentagon."

"Do you mean should you boil some water and make that oatmeal in case I don't catch a fish?"

I told him I couldn't have said it better. The earnest young provider studied the river and made a decision:

"Why don't you warm up the oatmeal while I go fish."

I thought this represented a compromise that two reasonable minds could live with. I walked back to the fireplace and left the boy with the river. The oatmeal was about ready when the fisherman returned with the verdict that no more trout lived in the Temperance River. I nodded and said his findings confirmed something I suspected for a long time.

Right about there Jimmy decided it was time for a long howling laugh. The oatmeal was ready and won Jimmy's approval.

We struck the tent and cleaned up our camp. He was a fatherless boy but somebody, undoubtedly his mother, had spent good and important time with him. He was polite and thoughtful and knew about dealing respectfully with nature. He separated the charred wood pieces methodically and piled dirt on them. He put some waste paper into his little utility bag and then, while I was bagging the tent, he walked a few feet into the clearing to be alone with the stream and the morning sun in the woods.

"Isn't it pretty?" he asked.

I said it was. "What I like best," he said, "when you come here by yourself like we did, it makes you feel that this belongs to us. I mean not for good. Just for now. Isn't it crazy that some people can come here and make a mess and not really feel how good this is? I want to come here again, and I hope it's just like today."

I agreed. I told him the professors who know about the environment call it "stewardship," what he had just said.

But Jimmy said it better.

In the years since then, I've tried a dozen times to locate Jimmy, through the organization that brought us together and through others. I've never succeeded. I don't know what became of Jimmy, where he is, who he is. I do know that there were two teachers on that weekend of ours in the north country, and I'm the one who probably learned more.

3

A Robinson Crusoe of the North
Meets Howling Wolves on a Frozen Lake

When we say wilderness, we're probably being more poetic than eco-
logically accurate.

There IS wilderness on earth, of course, strictly defined as a place where
no humans live. But we're not likely to see much of it in our lives unless we
find a place, reasonably accessible, where for at least a few weeks or months
there are—

No humans.

I rolled that idea around in my head when I was approaching the first
slim shadows of middle age. What kind of experience would it be, even in
a short term, if I found a place I could explore alone, make discoveries and
absorb sensations not felt before, far removed from the sound of human
voices and the sight of another human face?

The idea amused me at first. What are you going to be, some kind of
Robinson Crusoe in the jack pine forest?

But I thought a little further. Alone in a wilderness, no human sound
or face. I'd never had the experience, nor had many others, because human
beings historically have arranged themselves in large clumps of together-
ness that we call towns and cities. These often subdivide into congregations,
unions, coffee klatches and barbershop quartets. We are social creatures
because in an inarguable way we need each other.

Accepting this, I got out a map. I'd need a part of the world reasonably
accessible—I'm not talking solitary hiking in the middle of the Sahara—
where for a few days there was no likelihood of encountering another

human. What kind of animal life would you encounter and, if it came to that, how would you deal with it? How would you deal with the aloneness psychologically? Let's say three days of it. A taste.

I wasn't thinking a stone-cold, solitary-confinement kind of isolation. Rather it would be a foray into a part of the world, a wilderness at least in season, where there would be living things to observe, weather to react to, a compass to steer you and a stomach to feed. But you would be alone, free to explore the landscape by your own devices, in your time and impulses and with whatever resources and curiosity you would bring with you. You could do this unencumbered by timetables, alarm clocks and telemarketers.

Admitted, there is not much pure wilderness left in the industrialized world. There is, in fact, almost none if you define wilderness as a place inhabited only by wild animals or as a wasteland of desert. If you live in Minnesota, though, there is a place that for at least two or three months of the year, in mid-winter, qualifies as near wilderness.

The Boundary Waters Canoe country in the Minnesota northwoods spreads from Lake Superior north and west to the iron mining ranges. In the heart of it you can find isolation if you want it. For one astonishing interlude at night you can literally live with the wolves.

As a boy I lived in the town of Ely, right on its edge. There were no snowmobiles then. Skiing was considered a quaint and elitist sport undertaken only occasionally as a gesture to appease homesick Norwegians. The primary winter sport was ice fishing on Shagawa Lake, which in summer was the Miami Beach of Ely. The winter fishing was a serious, nose-numbing survival of the fittest, innocent of any pretense of the comfort that we have in the two-room portable manors that we call fish houses today.

But even today, if you go deep enough into snowbound forests of the Boundary Waters, you are going to be alone, and it is a good idea to do it carefully. You are probably not going to get eaten by wolves, but you are almost certainly going to encounter them. A suddenly-annoyed moose will pose a more practical hazard. And in those days so would the lack of communication with the outside world in an emergency, because the cell phone marvel then was still tumbling around in the brain waves of the wizards of Silicon Valley and elsewhere.

But the obvious dangers notwithstanding, I found the idea of facing true wilderness too attractive to resist, and one February morning I packed my sleeping bag, tent, mini-cooking stove, a pair of skis and snowshoes, packaged food, and a first aid kit, and headed for East Bearskin Lake in midst of the Boundary Waters.

In summer the Boundary Waters are the settled habitat of the recreational canoeist and the loon-seeker. Traveling alone in the same country in the winter takes a different orientation of the mind and different allowances for the flesh. By most of the conventional rules of touring and wayfaring, it's an unnatural act. There's some risk in case of an injury and clearly some discomfort. But I judged that those risks are marginal if the traveler is equipped and reasonably seasoned.

In a half hour of comfortable skiing on snow and occasional patches of bare ice, I put the lakeside cabins of East Bearskin Lake behind me. I was headed toward what my map told me would be a serviceable campsite between Alder Lake and Canoe Lake. The backpack was heavy but not oppressive. The body's adrenaline in the early going easily overcame the weight. I felt strong. If you want the truth, I felt completely elated. I stopped every ten minutes and filled my head with this rarest of all luxuries, scene after scene of winter wilderness—the frozen lake, the soundless forests on its flanks—and nothing of the rest of the world in sight or earshot. The sun

had scrambled the clouds and opened up swatches of blue. When a light tailwind came up at midday, I was virtually flying. The pack on my back actually gave some kind of aerodynamic lift.

The world's oddest spinnaker, I thought. I installed my tent on the snow of what in summer was a canoeing campsite. I got the little Optimus cooker going to melt snow for drinking water and then struck off inland to explore by snowshoe. Some old moose tracks plodded through a bay nearby and a weasel's precise little prints laced the ice near shore. Into the woods, the wind was picking up. It whooshed through the pines with those shifting bursts of energy and mood that seem to give the wind an invisible personality. The temptation to imagine some kind of message in its sounds is irresistible. Can the wind sing a welcome? A warning? Then the tone grows a little more solemn, a private hymn I imagined but couldn't possibly interpret. That may be why the wind in the pines is so beguiling. With its sounds and tempos it seems to mingle a yearning of its own with the visitor's. So for me, in my fancy, the wind more than any other force of nature seems imbued with human attitudes and moods. It can tantalize or evade and then lapse into silence. And once you're at that point in your musings you have to stop and tell yourself: "Hey, it's just the wind. It's not a four-act play."

Without a scientist's eye, the lone skier or snowshoer is going to indulge these fantasies. A wolf expert like David Mech or a naturalist like Theodore Wirth can give a lecture on the move describing the terrain and the signs. Not having the precise eye of the biologist, in fact, might heighten the fun. In that innocent condition it's almost impossible to avoid looking at the sounds and sights of wild nature allegorically. Sooner or later we assign human values to the part of nature that is most important to us. The sun is healing or the thunderclouds are malevolent. The wind is saucy or benign. It's a harmless fantasy and, if so, what was the forest doing today when this lone visitor was tracking up the snow and looking around in such simple satisfaction? Inspecting behind all of the snags of windfall?

If you want the absolute truth, the forest was full of pranks and tease. An overhanging branch of a big black spruce forced me to duck as I passed underneath. If you don't mind, I made the move flawlessly, without touching a twig. I straightened up, totally pleased with my dexterity.

And then an unseen branch higher up filched my ski cap cleanly.

Was this some kind of reprimand? Did I commit a social blunder coming into this woodsy cathedral with my head covered?

Two yards farther on, a bough loaded with snow swatted me in the rump.

And on. In this rather blissful condition I erected my tent, and the night went well. It delivered cracking sounds in the forests, creating some mystery about the source, although there was nothing much to fear. I cooked Spam patties and rice, put some Kool-aid in my water bottle, read a paperback beneath the battery-powered tent lantern, slept comfortably in the sleeping bag and then made breakfast from some freeze-dried cereal after I dressed. A creek near the campsite offered open water for my cooker and water bottle for the trail. The sky opened up and shafts of the early morning sun bent their way through the woods. I strapped on my snowshoes and headed through the woods for Johnson Falls. It was my destination for the day, a waterfall rarely seen even in summer in this shadowed forest of fir and hardwood west of Pine Lake. It was new to me and so was the route. My explorings were complicated by the snow and ice that concealed the little creek draining the falls' basin. But there wasn't a hint of slush crossing the lake ice that took me into the forest. Snow crunched beneath the big webbed baskets of my snowshoes. The breeze was at my back again, crisp and encouraging. The auguries were so good and I felt so fit that I was tempted to jog on the snowshoes.

It would have been a mistake, because the first 400 yards of the first portage I encountered in the woods was clearly built for steeplejacks. The portage between Canoe and Pine Lakes had never been wildly acclaimed by canoeists. It is a grunt of Olympic dimensions, not the most arduous in the territory but safely in the top 10. Still, with most of my tent, most of my gear and all the rest of the impediments back at the campsite, it was almost a pleasure cruise. Beyond it the terrain leveled out. No, this was not pure wilderness. Loggers years ago carved up much of it, hauling out the marketable pine and leaving the blistered poor relatives. But the forest had grown back, and the two of us were alone—the woods and the curious pilgrim. I thought, what a marvelous gift, a day like today, moving through the thicket, hiking beside an invisible creek, invisible because of the snow cover. Unseen, it was still a faithful guide. As long as I heard the gurgling water beneath me, I was on track for the waterfall because the creek carried the runoff of the falls.

Once in a while, when it was moving rapidly enough and the snow canopy was weak, the stream burst into the open. It swished darkly in the shadows, and in the moments when it was exposed to the sun, it flung reflections with a glitter so sharp that they stung my eyes.

I went on and found trouble. There was no actual sign of the falls high up on the bluff where it showed on the map. And now the angle of the ravine through which the creek flowed steepened and the creek both disappeared and fell silent. The map also revealed a slough further up the gully. I snowshoed into the gully and looked up to examine the bluff again. Nothing. No sound. I trudged around. Maybe I had taken the wrong turn on this treasure hunt. I listened. Again. And there it was. A plopping and bubbling. The creek ran to the east, exactly where it should have been going if it drained the waterfall. I followed the gurgling. The sounds increased. Straight ahead in the forest I found the most enormous cedar tree I have ever seen, at least five or six feet in diameter. It was a kind of lodestone of the day because ahead of me, the bluff was covered with jade ice. It was the waterfall, hanging mute. It was cloistered under two feet of ice that descended to a rough grotto of stone and fir trees.

It was striking and unearthly and profoundly alone. If you moved closer you could hear rumbling under the icicles. But moving close meant you might be walking on some uncertain ice, so this was far enough. The waterfall was dormant and the creek subdued. This was winter in the northwoods. Its nature was still wild, but now it was nature in its privacy—except for a solitary onlooker who was leaving, but would remember this small and solitary search for a mystery waterfall. It was real, and worth all of the labor.

On the way back to camp I waved politely to a Canada jay that had been squawking and pestering me all the way into the ravine. I tipped my ski cap to the noisy kibitzer. You win, jay.

It had been a good day and I slept soundly in my snug goosedown cocoon. The weather stayed congenial the next day on the ski back to East Bearskin but the night overtook me well before I could make the lodge and I settled into my tent on the thick ice of a tiny inlet several miles up the shoreline. The woods were too dense to set up camp on land in the dwindling gloaming. I moored the tent to a small tree, ate quickly by flashlight, tucked the water bottle into the sleeping bag with me to keep it from freezing, and fell asleep quickly.

I woke once, checked my watch and slept again. At 10 minutes before midnight, the concert began. The long wailing howl of the lead wolf pierced the subzero and drifted from the ice of East Bearskin into the crowns of the Norway pines.

There is no sound that so starkly defines the winter wilderness as a wolf baying at night. For any human intruder within earshot, it stifles the breath and grabs the skin. It evokes a tormented loneliness and a sense of menace too vivid to be appeased by the calmer wisdom of the woods, that wolves have no special history of molesting humans.

That is romantic, but not altogether correct. A man lodged alone in his tent on a frozen lake could know all about the lore without being totally convinced. There were more than one, I learned, as the leader wolf's next howling recital was answered by the yapping and barking of the others in a kind counterpoint. I struggled out of my sleeping bag, unzipped the front panel of the tent and looked out across the ice to the east.

Under a nearly full moon they were in shadow in a bay, but their forms were visible. There were five or six, moving about. They must have been a quarter of a mile away. But think of it. Here was a wolfpack in congregation under the moon and the flaming starlight on a February night in the Boundary Waters. And we were just a little more than 90 linear miles from the brand-name shopping center on the edge of Duluth.

There was another howl, more yapping and snuffling. The temperature must have been 15 to 20 below zero, heading toward 25 below. No thermometer was necessary. The bite of pain in the fingertips, touching cold nylon and metal, was a credible substitute for mercury. So was the stiff hair in my nostrils and the stunning light show of the northern sky pouring down on the white velvet of the lake's snow cover.

The wolves stopped. Nothing moved or sounded over the great ice sheet of the lake and the forests beyond. Goodby wolves. For a moment there, I considered the wisdom of scientific wolf-watchers, some of whom believe that the moonlit wailing isn't wailing at all but rather a celebration of joy by the pack, a family sing-along. I zipped and dozed. Fifteen minutes later the howling resumed, an unearthly siren that seemed to fill my tent from a distance that could not have been more than 100 yards.

My God. They were in my front yard, just off the shoreline from where I was camped in front of a grove of cedars. The barking seemed more urgent. That might have been the power of suggestion but there was nothing imaginary about the decibel count. It was running off the charts. I tugged out of my sleeping bag again and trained my flashlight on my available armory: a Swiss Army knife and four aluminum mini pots from my cooking set. If it came to battle I was going to defend myself with four aluminum pots.

That prospect didn't seem to terrify my visitors outside. The yelping accelerated. I'm not sure whether they were motivated by curiosity or some prospect more grim, but I'll never know because in trying to unzip the front door of the tent again I set off a racket that scattered the wolves either in fright or bafflement. When I looked out on the frozen lake again, it shone innocently in the moonlight. That and nothing more. A few minutes later something did crack behind me. But the performer this time was the subzero air, creating its percussions with the saps and knots of the Norway pines.

When I walked out to strike my tent in the morning I did notice a sag in the rear of the tent. The support rope tied to the tree on shore was limp. Looking closer, I found that it wasn't actually sagging. It was broken. More accurately it was cut. Gnawed.

The snow around it was crowded with paw prints.

The wilderness, friend, may not be as remote as you imagine. But when you think about it, that may be something to cherish.

4

The Enigmas of the Land of Everest

There was a figure on the trail, threading through the rhododendron trees. I'd seen this before. The late afternoon sun was streaming off the fluted icefields of Themserku nearly two miles above me. Again, as before. The Himalayas were in repose. It was a marvelous moment of harmony in the mightiest of mountains. It was also uncanny.

I had lived a moment exactly like this eight years before.

I watched as the scene enfolded, predictably. "He's going to stop at the next switchback," I told myself, "and he's going to duck under those rhododendron branches like the kid did eight years ago, and wave."

He did. The hour was the same as eight years before. The scene was the same So were the movements of the two figures, one sitting on a huge boulder above the river, me, the other ascending the trail to Phortse. It was a frame-by-frame reenactment of the episode in my life years earlier, an almost absolute duplication except for the face of the hiker on the trail. Years before it had been the face of a boy who materialized on the trail with his parents, waking me out of a nap on the flat-topped boulder where I'd gone to rest. But today it was an old man.

Every other detail and movement was predictable. The figure was no apparition. The face belonged to a Sherpa guide I knew named Pemba. I could predict what the old man was going to do next, as though some quirk of time and motion had extracted an episode from my earlier travels in the Himalaya and renewed it before my eyes.

I have to make a disclaimer here. In my professional life I spent more than forty years in daily newspapering, a very long hitch. I loved almost

(Left) Once beyond reach to the adventurer, Everest has now become a magnet for climbers and trekkers. It is never easy for either. But many return, again and again. To them, it becomes a kind of renewal.

every day of it. And it was a workout, a daily exposure to the full range of humanity's saints and con men, heroes, altruists, comedians, crooks and imposters, all of this fondly remembered. One story I heard more than once told of some remarkable repetition of the same event in the life of the teller. I always listened to these stories with interest. The inexplicable side of life is rarely dull. Still, I seldom found enough traction in those stories to write them. But here in my own life was a moment I literally *had* experienced before. Not in every minute detail, but close enough so that I found myself a step ahead of the action the whole time the old Sherpa was making his way up the slope. He will stop here, I said. And he did. Sometimes it was not on a switchback, but in the middle of the trail in a clump of rhododendrons where there was no opening, only a big rock. "He's going to stand up on the rock and look around," I said. "Right THERE."

And he did.

So what was this? Some old tapes, something else, playing with my mind? And then it dawned on me where I was. This was the Himalaya, where the chants of the Buddhist and Hindu mantras roll pleasantly and endlessly against the western ear in a strange, numinous tapestry of sound and supplication that seem to unite the ages. It's as though spirits and deities and legends are being summoned to fill the air above this great uplift of granite and ice. And there are times when you are not always sure what is reality and what is illusion.

But sitting 40 feet above the trail on this enormous boulder beside the Dudh Khosi River, I had no doubt that I could foretell the old man's movements. Eight years earlier the boy had done the same. I'd climbed up on the boulder a half hour before our evening meal in camp beside the Dudh Khosi. The sun's reflected rays off the Thermserku glaciers had produced a glorious light show in the late afternoon. I dozed for a few minutes and then was awakened by sounds from the trail 40 feet below. The boy was following his parents on the way from their potato patch. He began waiving as he progressed up the hill. I waved in return. By the time he reached the top of the slope we were friends.

And now it was Pemba, who was not normally a demonstrable man; not a kid, but acting like a kid. Nothing had changed. Afterward I did some calculations. A) The mind is fully capable of overreaching when it encounters simple coincidence, but B) How much do we really know about what we call coincidence and C) I recalled a conversation in northern Minnesota years before with a gentle old American Indian. The talk got around to spirituality, his and then mine. He asked about my religion. It was a gesture of courtesy. What he really wanted was to talk about his own spiritual life. He said millions of people who came out of cultures similar to the American Indians had a philosophy about time—that events and ideas had a great circular movement through the ages.

That philosophy, I knew, is also prevalent in belief systems in Asia and elsewhere in the world. My Indian friend believed that the whole pageant of life moves in cycles, uniting us with the past, actually and mystically explaining the past, sometimes duplicating the past and directing the future. He said this might partly explain why there are spasms in our lives when we seem gripped by instant recall or Deja Vu—that we have lived this experience before—and because we have, we can sometimes actually predict what will be said next or happen next.

I said I'd experienced those moments without connecting them with my religious life, which I admitted was basically mainstream Christianity. I believe in one God who created the cosmos and who was more or less stuck with the responsibility for all that happened afterwards. I believe that Jesus Christ was a man who appeared on earth as a kind of personification or revealer of God and changed the world. I believe in a form of afterlife, but I have no concept of what that means in my life today and in the hereafter if and when I enter it. I believe that the most sublime gift to humanity is conscience, which I take as a divinity within us. I believe it grants us free will to make the moral or immoral decisions we make, based on our values and whatever rules of morality or self-interest we adopt.

But the philosophy of a circular movement of ideas, faith and life itself is fascinating: the belief that the great turning movements of the heavens connect us with other times, merging our lives with those of the peoples of the past, the struggles of the past and the lessons of the past. Some tribal societies, whose spiritual life is linked profoundly with nature, are attracted to this belief. Some Eastern religions are also drawn to the mysteries of this philosophy. Some see it as the touchstone in our understanding of life. I look on it with respect. But I've found it elusive.

I find it less elusive today after that simple little scene in the Solu Khumbu of the Himalayan mountains, where Everest rules in its ancient garments of Chomolungma, which is what the Tibetans and Buddhists call "The Goddess Mother of the Earth."

The chance meeting with the Himalayan boy had moved me in a new direction in my experience in these mountains. The relationships I had acquired, with the Sherpa guides, their families, the condition of the villagers and their own yearnings made my ensuing journeys there more meaningful than the raw excitement of going higher and higher in those most magnificent of mountains.

On that day we had camped beside the Dudh Khosi and it was late in the afternoon. The Sherpa cooks would be serving supper in half an hour. I walked up the trail beside the river. The gigantic boulder beside it almost swallowed the trail whole. It sat like a huge black potato, three stories high with a flat top and enough gouges and seams to make it easily climbable. I was up in a few seconds. The sun's rays ricocheting off Themserku's ice were blinding and rather quickly made me drowsy. The beat of the Dudh Khosi's whitewater was hypnotic. So was the solar blaze on the Themserku's glaciers. I struggled to stay awake but finally blanked out. After a few minutes I was roused by sounds on the trail beneath me. A Sherpa couple was coming home from the family's little potato patch near the river. Potatoes grow at 12,000 and 13,000 feet in the Himalayas. Not much else does. The man carried two sacks of potatoes and the woman hauled their tools. Behind them walked a kid about five years old. His brown hair flopped around his face and as he came even with the boulder he looked up with his big dark eyes and saw me sitting on the top flake, spruced up—it must have seemed to him—with Vibram soled boots, knee-high gaiters and all the duds you buy at REI before flying to Kathmandu.

The kid stared, standing still. He rubbed once at his nose and kept staring. I may have been the first westerner he'd seen. He regarded me as you would an alien duck squatting in a crow's nest. And then as his parents headed for the bridge across the Dudh Khosi, the boy raised his arm cautiously. He waved. I waved and said, "Hi, little boy." At the bridge he turned and waved again, and I did the same. On the far side of the bridge he waved once more. I responded. The trail to the family's home 500 feet above the river in the village of Phortse wound through the forest of huge rhododendron trees, elegant and red with blossoms that eventually would paint the entire slope. Because the slope was steep, the trail reversed itself several times and at each switchback, the boy turned to me and held up his arm. He was clearly excited about making contact with this odd creature on the rock. Our mutual waving got to be very emphatic and almost aggressive. I could see the grin on the kid's face despite the growing distance. Until then the parents had been unaware of the kid's discovery, but at the top of the slope the mother looked behind her to the son, and then across the river to me. She lowered her head and spoke to the boy, who then turned very slowly as though suddenly changing attitude. He held his hands together and placed the fingertips to his lips. I couldn't hear, of course, but I knew what he was saying.

He was saying "Namaste." In Nepali, the word Namaste is a lyrical, all-purpose expression that can mean hello, thank you, you're welcome and how are you. But in its deepest spiritual sense it is one person's salute to the soul that resides in the other. It means, "I praise the God within you." It is the most beautiful word I know. It makes the day worthwhile simply knowing there is such a word. And because it is the word travelers from all lands use when they meet a stranger on the trail in the Himalayas—Nepalese, western, eastern, it doesn't matter—I stood up on the rock, placed my hands to my lips and said "Namaste."

And at that moment there was a connection.

The aging westerner on the trail and the brown-haired kid living a barely subsistence life in Phortse in the Himalayas were greeting each other in the honor of the same deity they worshipped by different names.

We were together. Consider. The God within you. Most people of faith probably would not put a construction that profound on how their God dwells in their life. But if you truly believe, that expression—the God within you—requires no philosophical stretch at all when you think about it. What it says is: There is something divine within us. And how do we identify this divinity? Let's consider that. We have an instinct to know right from wrong, to share or not, to serve or to indulge ourselves. We have the power within us to befriend or to estrange. We can love or hate. The path to goodness, to decency, is open to all of us, whatever our condition in life, and if that is not the god within us it is as close as we're likely to come to recognizing the spirit of God as we understand God. And this is what stirred me at the moment the boy and I stood facing each other with our fingertips peaked under our lips across a Himalayan gorge. We lived a half world apart, he in a scrabbling, grinding existence at nearly 14,000 feet in the highest mountains on earth. I lived in the most prosperous land on earth. There was an enormous gulf between us culturally, geographically, and generationally.

Yet we spoke to each other with mutual acceptance, across time and the continents. I stored the experience and found myself irresistibly drawn to that large boulder on each of my subsequent visits to the Khumbu. It was on one of those return visits that Pemba made his unexpected appearance in the rhododendrons.

Each time I've gone to the Himalaya I brood a little on the last day. I may not be back and that possibility somehow scares me. I'm not thinking about mortality. Age, yes, other needs, the simple arithmetic of the demands and choices in our lives, other places, other times, the people in our lives. I don't fly off in any maudlin exercise in manufactured grief. But this is a part of the world that has stuck in my marrow and steadily fuels a yearning to reunite with it and its faces and its starlight; the silence and the chill of dawn and the immaculate sky, slowly bringing warmth and renewal, and the remembered hubbub of my companions on the trail.

I admit it becomes a kind of fixation. The high country has a power that brings me—and I'm sure others-- close to a feeling of proprietorship. Earlier in my life I traveled to the Tetons of Wyoming where I hiked and climbed for 15 years. The sensations I felt in those travels lingered for months after the climbs, both as a memory to cherish and a prod to renew the relationship. So that each time I walked through the corridor of pines off the Signal Mountain road, and looked out on the Grand Tetons by starlight, I was fired by this sense of union. The Grand, Teewinot, Symmetry, Moran, Cloud Veil Dome, they were mine, ours, reaching back to the times I climbed on their cliffs with friends who knew the same sensation. I wanted to come back to embrace the mountains and the faces and voices they evoked. And looking up on those rock walls and snow ridges, I tingled and ached to be on one of those ridges right now, waiting for the exploding sun.

I need to assure you these feelings do not rise to the level of a neurosis. They were enrichment in my life; I was moved and somehow felt enlarged by the experience, and needed to renew it.

Later in life, the Himalayas exerted the same kind of allure, stronger because of their other-worldly remoteness, their immensity, and their mysteries. This is a land that mingles the roar of waterfalls with the chants of cloaked monks. It presents the visitor or the pilgrim with the treasure of some of the world's greatest natural spectacles, ironically linked with the poverty in the city streets miles away and on the hillsides. And for the trekker and climber, it forges a partnership with the tireless and companionable Sherpas, so many of them full of whimsy and the rhythms of their native dances.

And then there is the icon of Everest. Maybe that deserves an aside here: The mountain was identified in 1852 as the highest on earth, more than 29,000 feet above sea level, by the English surveyor general of India—an Englishman named George Everest. And so it became Everest. In North America the highest mountain became McKinley, named for an American president who had nothing remotely to do with the mountain. Years later people with enough sense to recognize that odd miscarriage successfully campaigned to restore the evocative name of Denali, the native Athabascan word for The Highest One. It's too late to change Everest. The very word has now become magnetic, invoking the image of the mountain's great power, uniqueness and hazard. But wouldn't we understand a little more humanely the mountain's place in the lives of people who know it best if we kept the Tibetan word of Chomolungma, "Goddess Mother of the Earth?"

This is Nepal's Solu Khumbu, where I've returned to travel often for more than 25 years—there and in the Annapurna Range to the west. The Himalayas are mountains for the mystics, for the hard-driving goal setters, for romantics, vagabonds and for the thousands that come to them each year wanting and needing to see the most magnificent high country in the world. The country is so high that it seems part of another world, an impression intensified by the sight of hundreds of prayer flags crackling on the ridges, rows of religious mani stones dividing the trail, and the lyricism of names the Nepalese and Tibets have given their mountains—Ama Dablam, Pumori, Lohtse, Machapuchare and Annapurna, the Goddess of the Harvest.

At first these mountains served as a sanctuary and a mirror where I could discover my strengths, fulfill my dreams, and soothe the guilts occasioned by my rather raw and active ego. Later they became a retreat where I could express a mellower self that had been so long in arriving. I could feel cleansed by these mountains and give thanks for that. As I grew older the Himalayas became the secret garden lifted from my childhood. I climbed there two or three times and trekked year after year, long after I had put aside thoughts and schemes of reaching their highest summits. They were mountains where I could wander without fear through a nature grand and beautiful and also, I noticed as I matured, so congenial. I discovered something in the songs and banter of the Sherpas, in the brown saucer eyes of the children of the mountains, in the bowed heads of the old women hauling firewood in their bamboo dokos, seemingly sightless and numb in the monotony of their labor. I felt a guilty sympathy for these outwardly fragile women, and whenever I stopped on the trail to say hello, they paused and straightened themselves, rewarding my whole day with a luminous smile that seemed to declare "Life is OK. Thanks for stopping."

Life has burdens, they seemed to be saying. Ours are different than yours.

Yes, they are. But in the Himalayas they were hardly burdens. We were 20 trekkers on our way back to the airstrip and Lukla and then to Kathmandu. If I had any burden as the escort it was trying to avoid damaging somebody's health or pride, if the height or exertion were starting to wear on them. Mine was trying to sift out the joys and unknowns of a change in my life ahead. So I would sift and imagine. And eventually, in rhythm with my slow, trudging pace up the mountain trail, I would lose myself in the cadences of my thoughts: trying to fathom the future, giving thanks for this moment of time, watching the great lammergeyers soaring overhead as they winged toward the Tyangboche Monastery, staring down at the thin ribbon of the Dudh Kosi 4,000 feet below. Adjusting my pack.

Some burden, I thought, compared with those of an old woman carrying the doko.

But the old woman knew all about that. Her smile might have been telling me, "OK, you have money and I have nothing; and maybe you worry more than I do. But when we stop and say hello, we're the same. Namaste."

The highest and mightiest: Everest in the Himalayas. Tibetans and Nepalese have another word: Chomolungma, Goddess Mother of the earth.

I don't know anywhere but the Himalayas where I'm gripped by that feeling of instant bonding between two people a half world apart. Across that immense distance in our material status, she would smile through her grime and sweat. I felt humbled and better to have met her. I thought then that such feelings would last for a few seconds of reflection, but I have found that they have become quietly but permanently ingrained in my life, and forever join me to that part of the earth, not so much sentimentally but as a recognition that this truly was a grace that entered my life.

We were in each other's lives, for one brief interlude in her's perhaps. For me, a lifetime. The faces I see in the Himalaya never fully disappear. They are a shifting gallery of my memories, orchestrating the echoes of villages called Khumjung, Kalapani, Pheriche and more. They evoke that indelible moment in the early morning when the sun lifts itself in its full warmth and magnificence above the crest of Nuptse and fills the great amphitheaters of the Himalaya with its benediction. And on the trail to Pangboche we will have to stand aside while a small caravan of yak passes us on its way to Everest's Base Camp. Behind all of that shagginess and procession of horns is the yak driver, snapping the herder's quirt against the sacks of flour on the yak's back, and bellowing "Yahhhk." He is scowling and ragged but when he passes me on the trail I slap him on the back and greet him with my most elegant French "*Bon jour, monsieur.*" And he looks up and laughs and winks, because we both know he's not very elegant and I'm not very French.

My laughter is saying something else. "I don't know you, but I wish I did. Maybe you're a rascal and maybe you're a village wiseman, but either way you're a poster of a beautiful day in your mountains and I want you to know how much joy it brings to me."

But there was also a postscript for me: how am I going to translate poster into Nepali? So the colony of yaks trudged by and the herder disappeared around the bend where the ravine opened up to the scrub pastureland beyond Pheriche. The wind picked up, he rammed his wool cap down below his ears and, just before he disappeared around a hay shack he turned back to me and yelled "Yahhhk."

Which made me one of the boys. I don't know if it's their Buddhism or their uncomplaining acceptance, but from a wellspring deep in their culture the Himalayans face hardship with a kind of weather-beaten dignity. Maybe the explanation goes deeper and maybe it's simpler. The poor know better how to survive. Those who have more to lose struggle more frantically to hold onto it.

Why return?

Why not. The monasteries? Yes, that. The Sherpas with their mumbled mantras on the trail, the prayer flags snapping in a half dozen vivid colors from a pole in the village centers, or spread above the mani walls in ribbons of white. All of that. The vastness of the landscape seems filled from horizon to horizon with the vibrations of something beyond.

But perhaps symbolically here in a part of the world where beauty coexists with the hardest realities of life, you will find nothing graceful about Everest. It is enormous and stark and emits a kind of distant, glowering hostility—if you let yourself fall into the old trap of attributing human attitudes to inanimate nature. But what *is* full of grace is the infinity of the Himalayan tableau, the mountains, the blue ice and dazzling snowfields, the sounds of the Dudh Khosi, roiling white and turquoise nearly a mile below, bearing the melted ice of the glaciers of Cho Oyu and Everest. But when you sit for a few minutes to watch the women swinging their hoes in the potato fields, you will often be favored by the scent of the juniper incense burning beside their garden patches. It is a rare and lovely snapshot to carry away, a time of peace and family in the Himalayas.

Sometimes it's a relief and delight to simply withdraw into humility and to feel yourself being pulled into some cosmic stream of time that connects the heavens with the tread of humanity.

And here it is. The mountains themselves seem unearthly in their sculpture and stupendous size, yet the scale of the Himalayas is so huge that Everest itself does not overwhelm the onlooker until it is a few miles away, erupting black and silent and fearsome above the Khumbu icefall. And then if fills the sky and one must close his eyes momentarily in the presence of a nature so mighty. And what else?

A nature so full of grace.

Prayers ripple in the breeze at the monastery of Tengboche.

5

Consider a Possibility: There IS a Heaven on Earth

"In these wilderness areas, we will find, if we have the heart, both spiritually and physically, to journey into the back country, that where there are no roads, only footpaths of the deer or made by the feet of men, we will come into an area that is virgin, that is holy... where the breezes bring you instructions if you listen to them properly."

– Flower A. Newhouse, *Springtime's Festival*

There are people whose minds and hearts ride the wind in search of an ultimate spiritual fulfillment. This they can only achieve by uniting themselves with a place or mood in nature so inspiring that it will serve them literally as a heaven on earth.

They may not be sure what, if anything, comes after their allotted time here on the rotating planet, where waves of prophets over the centuries have preached about the wages of the good life and the bad. They *are* sure about a time or place here on earth that needs no golden gates or battery of harps to tell them. "for you, it will never get better than this. Treasure these moments."

Let's say you are one of these; your spirit is tuned to special and inimitable places that can be wild or restful. Their very names ignite a sense of longing. The mood they create lifts you to an absolute harmony with your world, a feeling you can experience no where else.

Patagonia is one. Antarctica is another.

They many not be everyone's grail of discovery. But here is a Chicagoan named Joan Larsen, for whom the wild terrain of South America's peninsula and the frozen vastness of the Antarctic continent have taken her to the edge of what she calls "forever."

There is another way she might say this:

"As close to heaven as I may ever come."

And if you suspect that the heaven of the scriptures for some reason is not available—if, as Peggy Lee sang, "that's all there is,"—then what? Then the Patagonias, sunsets over the acacias in Africa, the rhythms of the ocean surf at night, are sights and sounds and sensations that millions in our midst want to experience and want and need to renew.

On the other hand, it may be altogether possible theologically to have that and heaven, too.

Introductions need to be made here. Joan Larsen is a traveler, amateur balloonist, writer, library advocate, hyperactive senior, and an inveterate explorer of the human condition. Somewhere on the fringes of that is the energizing drive of her personal philosophy: This is the one and only brass ring we're going to have on this planet. Take it and go. Search. Embrace the earth.

She became one of the most passionate and relentless advocates I have ever encountered of the power of wild nature to expand and actually trans-form our lives. For how long?

For Joan Larsen it can be one moment of total serenity, or a lifetime.

We began corresponding when she visited relatives in St. Paul years ago and read a piece I wrote about a climb in the Tetons. She asked questions from St. Paul and later from Park Forest in Illinois where she lives. What were my truest sensations during the climb, on the summit, on the descent? How would I compare them? With what?

"With Beethoven's Third Symphony," I wrote.

"What part?" she answered.

That kind of mind.

Over the years she had read the works of the Sufi poet Rumi, the natural-ist Paul Brooks, Joseph Campbell and more. She had traveled to Antarctica and to as far north as she could reach without a dogsled. She had walked in the gales of Patagonia and she'd watched the sunset over the Alaska Basin in the Tetons.

And then she would tell me, and her ever widening network of corre-spondents on the Internet, what was impelling her.

"There are some places we go not only to rest or to slow the march of time," she said, "but to make a pilgrimage into one's self. We experience a sense of forever. There are some places that in one burst of clarity bring us to an understanding deeper than anything we have ever known.

"I don't have to think or analyze or question the path. I call it a sanctuary...a power of place. It is a landscape of the soul. If we go on a journey outside the frenzies of modern urban life as lone pilgrims we give testimony to the power of this planet's beauty and of the human spirit that is so vulnerable to its spell.

"Each time I return to the beauty of Chilean Patagonia, a part of me says that I will never feel this alive again: The massifs of Torres de Paine, set off with snow and ice, rose-colored with jet black tips, the murmur of the wind and then the incredible stillness that is broken only by the sound and sight of condors overhead...small icebergs floating on the lakes the color of glacial blue. And the red foxes and ostriches, flamingos and parakeets...the place is primeval, almost untouched. And one day I placed two stones at the base of one of the spires. I engraved one with my name and the other with the name of my dearest friend, a person so in tune with the spiritual world, that the stones would, I knew, be there for all eternity. How could there not be a sense of peace, of completeness, at that moment?"

But Antarctica?

She finds that part of the world compelling beyond all others, impressed by the power of ice to sculpt a kind of lonely, laconic beauty that reaches into the heart of those who search the world for a personal and renewable bond with nature.

Joan Larsen: "I can look at a globe and see the tiny dots of islands, perhaps not named on the map of either pole, that I have managed to reach. Why would I go and then feel I had to return? I know the world pretty well. But there are only two places, Antarctic and Patagonia, that exert an almost magnetic pull.

"It's knowing you are at a place that touches your heart in a way that you couldn't have imagined. You are drawn back. Can you imagine being the first on earth ever to put footsteps on a place, so pure and pristine and beautiful. And I can bring it up in my mind at will, and actually "be" on the Antarctic ice again."

In Norway, hikers can season a day in the mountains with mythology. This is the route above Lake Gjende that Ibsen's Peer Gynt took down the Besseggen Ridge, riding a reindeer.

That is commitment. And what is the hard core impulse that stirs in the Joan Larsens of the world?

"I think life is what you put into it," she said. "I don't think you can just lie back and things will happen to you. You make them happen. You give it your all—and wondrous things happen every day. Life isn't dull and it never has been. I don't look back…what attracts me, every day, is what lies around the next corner."

The next corner. In that, she and I and probably you are akin, as long as the inviting corners don't intrude on some of the more urgent needs and demands of our lives.

But let's say we turn that corner some day, and find a place and a moment so rare that it surpasses all prior moments, and we find ourselves experiencing something close to the tranquility and bliss that have been offered to us as the reward for faith and good works here on earth?

"For Paul Brooks, the writer and naturalist," she said, "the concepts of heaven were somehow associated with wilderness. Heaven was not a garden or necessarily a Christian heaven with billowy clouds. It was not even the paradise of monotheistic religion. For him the afterlife lay at the end of a hard, three-day hike to a high, blue lake surrounded by snow-covered mountains. It's here that you strip off your clothes and dive into the lake. You build a fire and eat fresh trout, you watch the gold of the afterglow on the snowy peaks beyond, and then you sleep the sleep of the righteous in this wilderness." The Persian poet Rumi also looked at the wilderness as such a transporting place. He described wilderness as a clarity of vision, a wide, select emptiness where, alone in the world, you experience a peace that passes all understanding. It is here that all questions are answered or rendered superfluous.

Well, yes, although I'm not sure about reaching the first rungs to Nirvana by frying a trout and diving naked into a mountain pool surrounded by snowbanks.

The reality is that each of us seeks the spiritual differently. Yet the enhancements we find in nature are part of this quest and are commonly felt by most of us. The search for spirituality, a kind of peace that moves us to a sense of well being, does not demand a specific belief in a higher power that created life in all of its forms. But the notion aggressively advanced by some of my friends—that there is some organic contradiction between (a) achieving spirituality and (b) spending an hour in a house of worship—is one where I generally change the subject to tomorrow's starting pitcher.

We define our own spirituality, as well as the intensity of it. Several billion people on earth profess a belief (which sometimes takes the form of a wish) in a creative, universal power, usually called God. This belief does not require an absolute adherence to what we call Scriptures. It does, though, make us think about tomorrow. It also assumes a certain level of behavioral decency and offers a code of conduct that includes service to those who have less than we have.

Almost none of this, while uplifting, is going to assure a certain level of serenity in our lives. We are mortal and imperfect. We are vulnerable to fear and we are often self-serving. We are, in short, human. Which is why the nature around us, for so many of us, comes to assume a significant and even transforming role in our lives. It can be sanctuary that seems to breathe peace into our minds and hearts. For many, traditional faith cannot or does not offer these things in comparable portion. But one does not necessarily have to replace that faith, or the yearning to have faith.

And for those we will present an exercise. Raise your hand if you've had this experience:

It's the middle of summer, work drags, lawn parties generate all the suspense and cultural improvement of the beer commercials. The news is about mayhem in the streets, another cable provider is either being sold or sued, and there is always the possibility of one more war on the horizon.

You haul a tent and sleeping bag with you and a portable cooker and you head for the woods. Or you rent a cottage or motel unit. Somebody hands you a map at the entrance to a state park. You strap on a pack and follow the arrows that denote "Hiking Trail."

(When I hike in the German-speaking countries, one word on a sign, "Wanderweg" quietly but suddenly ignites all of my anticipations connected with a walk in the forest. Simply, it means hiking trail. But the word "wander" for me translates into something broader—exploring, rambling, freedom. And let's go.)

So with pack and a light step you walk through the birches and pines, pause to watch some flower petals floating in a brook, and stand on a hill overlooking a lake where there is no sign of habitation, only a tiny wake of three ducks paddling in formation.

You do it again the next day. And by the time you're driving back to your home, something has changed.

It may be nothing very dramatic. The price of the gas you buy at the station may still be offensive, but not quite so offensive to require the usual four-letter rebuttals. Somebody is rattling on over talk radio, but after a 30 or 40 miles you might be tempted to turn it off and drive at a level of contentment you have not felt for awhile. You turn it off.

There is a pretty uncomplicated reason why you're likely to feel some quiet symptoms of fraternity with the world: fewer tensions; healthier attitude; yield the passing lane to the hard-charging NASCAR clone behind you.

The woods where you have walked have brushed you with a silent but undisputable healing force. Psychologists can explain it, but probably in language no better than yours. There are no disputes where you have walked. You feel a pervading quality of welcome there. The leaves of the aspen twitch in the breeze and somewhere distantly a woodpecker is yammering high on a tree truck. A few yards ahead the shade on the trail yields to sunlight, which momentarily glazes your cheek, and for a few seconds you close your eyes. You might be offering a prayer but you don't have to. And you want the trail to go on and on, because you're not tired. You feel no threat there, no confrontation.

Most people who worship have a second chapel where there are no stained glass windows. Yet it is a place where they sense God in a personal way. For millions, it is the good earth around us. A kind of non-denominational retreat. It can be a spectacle of nature but more likely a quieter place. The woods seem incorruptible. The hiker feels a kind of kinship with the forest and the streams, and then a comfort, and then a kind of cleansing that eases through the mind and body. He or she may be alone, but they do not feel alone.

If God is peace, why do we struggle so hard to understand what has happened to us?

There are some who are convinced that this kind of nurturing nature not only is a representation of God but a deity of its own in the reconciliation it achieves, the reverence it inspires and the wholeness it can create in the human spirit. Larry Gates, an authority on hummingbirds in Arizona, probed the literature of some of the great naturalists and writers who saw this quality of the oneness of humanity and nature. They have been drawn to the indivisibility of it, convinced that the power and grace of nature actually flow into your body and mind when you come to admire or discover. Some of these are mystics, convinced that nature itself should be the object of our worship.

You can argue that, of course. Trees live and die. Ocean surfs can become homicidal when they turn into tidal waves. Such pragmatists don't usually get very far with the lines of the poet Rumi: "I am the dust in the sunlight, the ball of the sun…I am the mist of morning, the breath of evening…the spark in the stone, the gleam of gold in the metal…I am the circle of the spheres, the scale of creation, the rise and fall…I am the soul in all…

John Muir, the great interpreter of nature and a godfather of the conservation movement, might bring us closer.

"These blessed mountains are so compactly filled with God's beauty, no petty personal hope or experience has room…the whole body seems to feel beauty when exposed to it as it feels the campfire or sunshine, entering not by the eyes alone but equally through all one's flesh like radiant heat, making a passionate, ecstatic pleasure-glow not explainable. One's body then seems homogeneous throughout, sound as a crystal."

Experiences like these may lead us to take a step backward and ponder the incalculable wealth available to us depending on how we approach the earth on which we live.

One day a letter from a 12-year-old boy named Gerald arrived on my desk at the newspaper. The boy read that the highest mountain in the world, Everest in the Himalayas, had been climbed in the 1950s. He was interested in climbing and wanted to know what goals there were for him now. I wrote to him as one who had climbed mountains, but who had never climbed the highest mountain:

"A boy doesn't have to climb Mt. Everest, Gerald, to feel the rewards of the mountains. There are mountains enough for your imagination and some day for your inquisitive spirit and impatient feet. You should not try to measure your reward by the height of the mountain or by the thrills you feel. You can learn to love the earth. And while you are doing it you will discover certain moments when you and the earth are united, when you feel you are part of the wind and the rock and you share their strength and beauty. And it will not be a moment for feeling awed or humbled or inconspicuous but for understanding that however we—or you—define God, there is a kind of divinity in this moment. You do not have to be alone to experience it, but perhaps you will be.

"There is a trail in the Grand Teton Mountains called the Cascade Canyon Trail. It lifts you out of the historic valley called Jackson Hole and into the core of the mountains. For three miles it carries you beside the jade stream, which sometimes swishes thoughtfully and sometime roars and charges. Later the trail rises out of the canyons and avalanche chutes and winds past a tiny lake called Solitude. It climbs the steep slope of granite and scree to a flat tundra. It is a barren place of glacial gravel, dwarf pine and struggling alpine flowers, called Paintbrush Divide. It's the kind of goal we can manage today on one last hike in the fall.

"Another day we can climb the mountains, when we have our equipment and time. But you do not have to reach the summit to deserve the special grace of this place. So we will hike it alone, a walk though the mountains and the Douglas fir and the swishing stream. We have no conquests today, no defying gravity. We can call it a small requiem of our own on the trail, one more season gone, with our thanks."

6

Traveling in Another World –

Geysers Erupt in Snowfields and the Earth Shakes Where Chief Joseph's Warriors Passed

We weren't expecting an earthquake when we skied through the heart of the grizzly domain of Yellowstone's Hayden Valley in the dead of winter.

We also weren't expecting to be measured for a head-on charge by two heavyweight buffalo. Nor could we have imagined a flourishing paradise of hot springs surrounded by snowdrifts six feet high.

But I don't know why we should have been surprised. No experience in outdoor America can quite surpass the sight of geysers erupting out of icefields and rivers floating through a prism of colors created by the runoff of dozens of hot springs.

In the more than 20 years since our extraordinary winter visit, the battles over the management of Yellowstone in winter have been waged at the highest levels of sanctimony on all sides. The contending interests are the snowmobile dealers, wilderness protectionists, tour agencies, bureaucrats, macho clans and cross-country skiers.

In a charitable mood, you might excuse them all for their conflicting postures of piety. The fight is over the wisest or the most popular (and profitable) use of a wildland resource that is almost too spectacular to manage in a way that will satisfy everyone.

The reason for it is right in front of you as you pass through the gateway of West Yellowstone, Montana. You're entering a huge and extraordinary theater of elemental nature in shapes and moods that thrust the geologic ages into the twenty-first century. It is a place where the spray of erupting geysers ices the fur of massive bison; and the trees are laced with filigrees of ice and frost. Mudponds gurgle and belch in temperatures of minus 30 degrees.

Some compromises have been reached in the years of skirmishing since four of us skied through the Hayden Valley in February of 1982. Some of the rules have been tightened, some loosened. But regiments of visitors have come and gone since then and I don't know that our week, which became both an idyll and a literal shock, could be repeated in all of its dimensions today.

We headed into the valley on skis in a fifty-mile-an-hour gale, and the sights came quickly. The first was a beast up ahead of us: He was bleeding. He must have been only a few hundred yards ahead, a buffalo laboring in the snow, coloring it with splotches of blood.

Now and then our skis glided over the fresh stains. From the rim of the valley where the forest of Douglas fir thrashed and creaked in the wind, a coyote barked. The west wind gathered thousands of tiny ice shards from the snow plain miles before us and drove them into our faces. The wind smelled of sulphur. It fumed from the hot-water stream that flowed through millions of tons of snow lying in the basin we were crossing.

Steam in the snow; a wounded buffalo struggling in drifts up to his massive shoulders; ravens circling; and not far behind, the river thundered and frothed through the Grand Canyon of the Yellowstone.

The mind spins when it is confronted with all of these colliding sensations and tries to assemble some order and reality out of them, in a place that seems lifted from another time and universe. Somewhere in the midst of all that sensual anarchy you have to ask:

Is there any place on earth as astonishing as the interior or Yellowstone in midwinter?

But Bill Stang is a man who manages to suppress most astonishments. He was a carpenter and contractor from Minneapolis, shrewd, earthy and weathered, and one of those rare creatures who derives his joys prowling the frozen wilderness of the world from Alaska to Arcadia.

"The buffalo may have lost a horn," Stang said. "Maybe it had an argument with another buffalo. Sometimes they rub against the timber to use the pitch for healing. Usually they rub just to get rid of the irritations. This one's not going to die. I doubt that we ever see it."

Hayden Valley is the wildest and most expansive section of the great wildlife preserve that is Yellowstone: in summer the habitat of grizzly, elk and buffalo, a vast marshland where the grass savannas flow like the surf and banks of steam from the fumaroles float above the timber.

In the winter of 1982 it was all but sealed to human visitation. The park services were allowing only a few hardy souls to enter. But it would not allow many because while the animals living there are huge and the weather is hard, the ecosystem is relatively frail. And so, sometimes, are the human visitors.

Two permits a month, the park ranger said. "That's about what we give. The weather is usually bad, so that figure is probably a little high. One guy has been through it this winter. A couple of weeks ago it was 40 below in there and another party was smart enough to come out."

The hundreds of buffalo live on the sedge they find by battering the snow with their mighty heads and by mooching the banks of the thermal streams, where the temperature stays constant at 50 degrees no matter how cold the air.

The grizzlies, of course, live wherever and however they want to. But although they have been sighted in January and February, in normal winters they are deep in hibernation. We allowed ourselves six days, from the road junction two miles north of Tower Falls in the northern part of the park, over the 8,800 foot Dunraven Pass to the Yellowstone Falls at Canyon 20 miles south of the junction, a quick ferry by snow machine to Alum Creek at the head of Hayden Valley and then the rest of the way by ski to Mary Lake at the foot of a mountain ridge and down the Nez Perce Creek to the road to Old Faithful. It would come to 50 miles by ski if we could accommodate the wind and the risk of breaking through ice and snow bridges over the creeks. There was also the possibility of dealing with annoyed buffalo and a dozen small catastrophes sprinkled unseen along a wilderness trail in winter.

None of that presented any serious hazard to safety. But there also was the obvious need for precaution in avoiding any needless intrusion on the wildlife and on any fragile thermal area we might encounter.

Our party was small but experienced and reasonably sound psychologically and physically: Doug Kelley and Rod Wilson are lawyers, Bill Stang, older and a relentless outdoorsman; I was a newspaperman and organizer of the trip and also more or less in charge of morale, the only requirement being to find a place to camp relatively secure from wandering grizzlies.

By noon of the second day we had reached the summit of Dunraven Pass in a high wind that turned the treeless plateau into a screaming white-

(Right) A skier looks out on the thermal theater of Yellowstone after crossing the Hayden Valley in mid-winter.

out. It also made hash of Bill Stang's lungs, because he was skiing on unfamiliar waxed skies and there was nothing in his pack to hold the slick snow we encountered on the steep grade to the pass . So he poled up on his arms and rewarded himself with an extra cut of Cervalat and four big handfuls of gorp when we got to the top.

A larger reward, an hour later when the wind slowed, was the sight of the huge Washburn caldera, revealed by the vague outline of a crater rim nearly 50 miles across where 600,000 years ago what may have been the earth's greatest volcanic explosion created the thermal system that draws millions of people to Yellowstone every summer.

But this was February. There were no tourist crowds or nature hikers in sight. If the Yellowstone interior fascinated you in winter, the trade-off was 50 pounds on your back, a cooker to thaw the freeze-dried food and melt snow for drinking water, knee-length gaiters and sleeping bags, a tent and what became the group's mantra in the morning:

"Don't let the snow bridge fall into the river. It's hard to ski in five feet of water."

And why struggle with Yellowstone in winter? Lord, why not? There is no winter like this one, where the geyser spray frosts the trees with Christmas flocking; the buffalo evoke the age of dinosaurs and the trumpeter swans float like snow queens.

Not far away, a petrified forest thrust its strange statuary above the snowfield, and the visitor could not resist the thought: This is how it might all have begun.

We left our second overnight in the park settlement of Canyon not far from the Grand Canyon of the Yellowstone, skied past Alum Creek at the valley entrance and into a southwest gale that swept ice crystals into our goggles and cheeks as we headed across a hard-packed windslab. It was nearly 10 miles across the valley to a neck in the forest where the trail to Mary Lake was blazed. But in the blowing snow we navigated by compass. It might as well have been marine navigation. The whiteout was that bad. The wind grew. After we encountered the first buffalo I removed my Gore-Tex mittens to adjust my camera, and the wind flung one of the mittens out onto the snowpack. It skittered and bounced and, with high determination and a tailwind, it headed for the road three miles away.

For the winter camper in a storm, a mitten is right up there on the value scale with family, God and credit rating. I shagged after the flying mitten with a full backpack. I didn't have the time to remove the pack because the mitten was on the edge of my sightlines. I chased it over the snow, around creeks and through the fractures in the snow and finally overtook it in a snag of dried sagebrush. I rejoined the others setting up camp in a clump of pines. We'd just finished when two of the hairiest buffalo we'd ever seen lifted their heads above the ridge, just ten feet away, and stared at us in terrible judgment.

We moved our camp.

And the next day, without warning from the volatile forces churning thousands of feet beneath us, the earth itself moved.

That morning we had stoked the hardy little cooking stove, 5 inches in diameter, melted snow for watery chocolate, boiled some sausage and freeze-dried oatmeal, and then skied off toward Highland Hot Springs miles away. To get to the intervening woods we floundered in soft snow up to the navel. Somewhere during those maneuvers I broke one of my fiberglass ski poles. I thought: there are worse calamities than a broken ski pole on a mountain trek where every stride needs leverage and support…but there aren't many.

Bill Stang examined the wounded pole and decided it might respond to trail surgery. In my pack was a plastic mess-kit knife, the kind that comes in the little leather pouch. None of us used a knife or fork for winter camping. One spoon and one eight-inch cup handled all of the nutrition from hot chocolate to lasagna. But Stang is that flower of civilization, the kind of handyman who could have fixed the Titanic with a hot patch and a pair of pliers. He turned my mess kit knife into a splint and strapped it to the pole with duct tape. When the duct tape was gone, we used adhesive tape. When Stang finished, the pole worked. And when Stang had vanished down the slopes, I examined the other pole.

It was broken six inches from the tip. I remembered Stang's ministrations with the other pole. By the time I reached the orange blazes marking the route into the timber and caught up with the others, I was the only skier in the Rockies carrying his knife on one pole and his fork on the other. And the poles were still intact when suddenly the snows parted and, through

a whorl of mist, we entered the pastures and sinter beds of Highland Hot Springs. You had to buck miles of snow and wind, and camp night after night in it, to appreciate the raw luxury of Highland Hot Springs. The normal procedure when you tent in deep snow is to stomp around on skis for half hour to create a platform. And when you get off your skis to prepare the sleeping bag and mat, you sink to the crotch in soft snow until it hardens from use. I'm speaking of the snow, of course. But these were actually hot springs, a little piece of Eden in the middle of miles of trackless snow. We didn't molest the springs. There was plenty of soft grass a hundred yards away on the perimeter, grass deep enough for a cows' picnic. Here, in the middle of Yellowstone in February.

"All we need," somebody said, "is an apple and a serpent." With the temperature in the tropical 40s outside, we had settled into our sleeping bags for a pre-supper nap when we felt the first rumble.

The feet seemed to tingle and movement rippled through our bodies. It was a shock, a faint one. The tremor continued. Two of us sat up. Somebody said, "are YOU feeling it?" Something deep below us seemed to be surging slowly. I stared at Kelley. Once every generation or so a quake hits Yellowstone with destructive force.

But within 45 seconds or so, the vibrations ended.

In the geologist's office at Old Faithful 20 miles away, the tremor was recorded on the seismograph, one of 18 to 20 annually registered on the Richter Scale there. This was the only Yellowstone tremor reported so far this year, the seismic watchers reported later. They logged it officially at 2.5 but offered wry congratulations. "It happened just a few hundred yards from where a 6.1 earthquake hit in 1975, and shook rocks and dust all over the Grand Canyon of the Yellowstone. You were camping right over the epicenter."

But there was no destruction on this night. Relieved, Doug Kelley strode to a snow-covered log, which he deemed qualified to serve as his dining room for the evening meal. Kelley anointed himself the supper chef early in the trip. He is a man of fastidious habits for a lawyer and did not argue with the group's consensus that he was a helluva cook with Rich-Moor's freeze-dried food. He looked on his kitchen duties with a sense of noblesse oblige. If a man is good, why suppress it? Most winter cooks will slap a pot on the roaring little cooker, melt snow in it, boil some water and pour it into the foil bags. Kelley spent time carefully creating shelves and counters in the snow. His reasoning was clear: you wouldn't ask a violinist to give a concert in a junkyard.

For tonight he chose beef Stroganoff, preceded by chicken-flavored noodle soup. It brought the expected sighs of adulation from his guests. But when one of us (alright, it was me) leaned against the snow shelf for support, Kelley scowled:

"You're about to sit in the dessert."

"I don't see any dessert."

"It's in the foil bag."

"I just see yellow glop," the boorish guest said.

"For God's sake, it's settling. Give it a half hour and it will harden into pie."

As the unregistered boor of the night, I peered into another foil bag. "What is this brown powder?"

"It's Graham cracker crumbs," Kelley corrected. "Just let me work, please."

The boor retired in proper disgrace. Actually, Kelley's blueberry cobbler the night before was pretty lousy. I would never have confronted him with that. He might have handed the apron and spatula to me, a sure ticket to starvation.

And in the morning we were off for the last day of our journey from the Dunraven to the civilized world, with some wistful feelings that were deepened when we skied through the Douglas firs and came to a marker beneath the timbered slopes of Mary Mountain. On this warm winter morning, with a snow shower frolicking impudently through the shafts of pale sun, the trail brought us to the memorialized agony of the march of Chief Joseph's Indians.

They had come this way in 1877. The new landlords of the mountain west had already created a national park out of this vast wildwood and grazing range, with its thermal theaters and June-in-January amazements. Even in its unexplored state Yellowstone was formally decreed—in all good conscience at the time—as a natural playpen for millions of tourists in generations to come.

Chief Joseph's Indians could not be reasonably asked to join in the acclaim. They had lived and hunted here for centuries. And now they were dying. They refused to accept consignment to a remote reservation that had no kinship to their history or the way they lived. Ahead of an American cavalry force, their dwindling caravan crept toward the Canadian border they would never reach. Their flight led them through the Douglas fir where Rod and Doug and Bill and I now skied in the sunlight on a lovely day. Many of Chief Joseph's tribe had died there.

There were no other human voices, no churning pistons. Apart from a tiny orange blaze set into a tree trunk every 50 yards or so, there was no intimation that the world of Yellowstone or the world at all was any more or less than it was a hundred thousand years ago. The wildness of it was total. Even the trail before us, an almost perfect trough about 30 inches across and two feet deep, downhill, might have been sculpted for skiing. It was not the grooming of a man-made machine, rather the work of prehistoric settlers—the buffalo that trudged this corridor in the winter on their way to the steam beds.

But in the fir forest there seemed to be a solemnity. Maybe the forest was imbued with some spirit of judgment. It might have something to say here, where so many had died in the midst of their long and tragic march.

If not the forest, then another Indian chief whose words seemed almost to whisper to the passing travelers.

His words are engraved: "Every part of this soil is sacred in the estimation of my people. Every hillside, every valley, every plain and grove, has been hallowed by some sad or happy event in days long vanished.

"The very dust upon which you now stand responds more lovingly to their footsteps than to yours, because it is rich with the blood of our ancestors and our bare feet are conscious of the sympathetic touch."

So the Yellowstone is not a museum. It is not the dioramas on the rim of the canyons or the nature trail guides who tell us about Yellowstone.

Yellowstone is the two great Douglas fir, standing mute here beside the trail. They are old enough to have absorbed the history. They can't talk. But they were here.

There was one more stream to cross before the road to Old Faithful. We'd become quite adroit about skimming across those snowbridges under the added weight of 50-pound backpacks. A probing ski pole could usually tell if there was enough snow to cross safely.

We were only an hour or so away, and the woodland seemed laced with a kind of droll hospitality, making mischief. The pine branches dusted us with snow crystals as we skied beneath them, the confetti of the forest. Sometimes they turned elfin, dumping dollops of snow on our heads without warning as though inviting the strangers to a snowball fight.

Don't tell me the forest is inert and oblivious.

And if the revelation of that was one more of its gifts on a memorable day, there was another: the gratitude it aroused in us for the gruff but valued company in which we traveled this road: Rod Wilson, who seemed never to harbor a mean or petty thought; Bill Stang, with his sourdough savvy and timeless exuberance, and Doug Kelley, with his strong, Green Beret will and his underdone blueberry cobblers.

Kelley dawdled at the last hot spring before we reached the road. He claimed camera trouble but that was a transparent cover. He didn't want to reach the road. The forest's benediction was that enduring.

But here was the road to Old Faithful after all. After we got there, we camped in the woods rather than checking into rooms in the skier's lodge. If you are spending the night a few hundred feet from the Old Faithful geyser, courtesy alone to this queen of Yellowstone's spectacles will stir you to walk by starlight to the viewing gallery in front of the geyser. At 4:30 in the morning, it is a private showing. Old Faithful rumbles and sighs and then lifts its fountain full, and sprays the night with ribbons and lace. It is the gift of Yellowstone in winter. A departing kiss from the prima donna.

7

Biking with Amy

One entry in my daughter's resume shortly after she finished college was a genuine eye-opener. It was preceded by more familiar recitals: honors graduate from Yale, the Law Review University of Chicago Law School and miscellaneous internships between school terms in the offices of Vice President Walter Mondale and the Minnesota attorney general. It also included doing grunt work with a highway department crew in summer to supplement her student loans.

To these was added: Bicycling 1,100 miles with my father from Minneapolis to the Grand Teton Mountains in Wyoming in 1981.

I can add a footnote to the last entry: Against the wind and 9,000 feet up.

We can argue which of these exertions best conditioned Amy Klobuchar for the Senate of the United States, although you don't want to underestimate strong quads and the ability to go four hours without water as a

© 2007 STAR-TRIBUNE, Mpls-St. Paul

qualification for the Senate. It's still in dispute whether the long ride west was her idea or mine. At various times we have both taken credit for it and denied complicity.

What I remember, beyond any dispute, is every mile of the 1,100.

I can't speak for the senator, which would be a presumption. The last time I sat in the Senate gallery she was serving as the Senate's interim presiding officer, doing such things as recognizing the senators from Connecticut and Tennessee. Not being a senator, I'm entitled to no such recognition from Madam President, which was how they were addressing the senator from Minnesota.

But from this distance of 26 years I remember every mile of that ride with great love, fondness, and a few cardiac tremors. I'm sure Amy would agree that none of those conditions saturated every hour of that week and a half, but they were ten of the most memorable days of my life. Day by day I discovered a young woman who, I realize now, I scarcely knew.

Approaching the crux of the ride the final day—Togwotee Pass above the historic Jackson Hole of Wyoming—I found myself regretting that it was almost over. I remembered the heat and wind, and our chatter, then sieges of silence when we were both tired or grumpy or not feeling well. I remembered our serious talks about the years ahead, abruptly interrupted on one occasion by a siren announcing violent weather, thunderstorms, high winds and probably hail the size of baseballs at Chadron, Nebraska.

Like any self-respecting expedition, we decided early on a distribution of work. On the road, I performed such acts as riding first to cut the wind, hauling the tent, knocking on farmers' doors for water, carrying the packs and providing money.

Amy was the navigator and radio operator. She handled the weather reports that squawked into her transistor radio, made scientific predictions, brought me up to date on her graduation agendas in the ivy parlors at Yale, and delivered announcements siphoned from the gossipy little radio stations of the West.

"Brian Atkins and Alice Moore are getting married Saturday near Chamberlain," she disclosed as we rode east of Winner, South Dakota.

"Good," I said. "Tell the newlyweds to honeymoon by bicycle."

"It's a great conditioner for marriage."

She was also the trip's conscience, and self-designated den mother and etiquette counselor, carefully protecting the family dignity .

"Dad," she said on the Dakota prairie, "I think it would be a good idea for you to change your T-shirt this afternoon."

"The odors of honest labor are nothing to apologize for," I huffed.

"It's just a matter of taste," she said. "Use your own judgment. I just don't want the farmers thinking that you're inconsiderate when you knock on their door for water."

I rummaged in my saddle bags for another shirt when we crossed the mile-long bridge over the Missouri River west of Platte, South Dakota. By then we had adjusted to the voltage of the prairie sun. In 500 miles our skins had acquired a becoming cast of chestnut. We had also acquired the Bedou-in's instincts for water conservation and were drinking in trickles instead of gulps. You had to do it. In South Dakota the commercial water supplies may be three hours apart for the bicyclist.

The agronomist sees the Dakota prairie as bountiful and unselfish, a giver of bread and beef for the world's lunchpails and its tables. The bicy-clist sees it as that, but he also sees it as an ant probably sees a football field. The land seemed to have no limits. It seemed, in fact, almost invincible in its raw geography. But the mathematics of our ride were pretty rigid. We had to average more than 100 miles a day on our timetable. If we ran into tornadoes, as we did at Vesta, Minnesota, or 35-mile-an-hour head winds followed by a one-hour hailstorm—as we did near Mitchell, South Dakota—the next day it would be 130 miles.

But it was not an ordeal. We rode the back roads, which meant hours for gabbing or introspection: For me, it also meant discovering a little more each day, in ways surprising, hilarious and sometimes moving, about a young woman I thought I knew well. I was fascinated by her matur-ing mind and by some of her intensities. Sometimes the discoveries were mildly jolting and often touching. For the first time in our lives we would talk for long periods about the world, its wonders, its injustices, and our place in it. We talked about her ambitions and her friends. I was pleased to see her compassions and loyalties, and surprised by the level of her anger at the pace of the country's reform to meet the needs of the neglected and abused. But she was fun and sometimes unpredictable, and she needled the trunks off me.

We had come all these miles together, and we were both older and younger for it. She had been a pixie and a scold and a soldier, laboring up hills for an hour at a time without speaking, and then bursting with chatter and plans. Not surprisingly, she was captivated by the big country. She had been there before, and this time getting there was the thing. Getting there on the back roads meant the towns were tiny and remote, and we were welcomed in each as visitors from another galaxy. It's not that these people don't watch television. They do know the world. But the land is their destiny, to be tilled and harvested. It is not for larking about the country and experiencing dust on a 15-speed bicycle. . The weather for us might have been a throwaway line or a simple inconvenience. For the farmers and ranchers it is their nurture and sometimes their demon. You can ride a bicycle through the countryside where nothing eventful seems to be happening. But it is here where a real America lives and harvests and worries about drought. And this realization helps to put the country in perspective for the traveler.

And what country!

Amy's health had improved by the time we reached Riverton, Wyoming. And she was singing cowboy songs she remembered from a "Sons of the Pioneers" record at home. And at that moment, when the western sky billowed over us like a gigantic umbrella of buttermilk, I simply gave thanks for being able to see and feel the American West astride a bicycle, which means you can take it in big gulps and watch the eagles and gape at the distant thunderheads and feel the power of it.

With the Tetons approaching we both felt a rising excitement and a kind of vulnerability in the presence of such mighty natural forces. When you drive west by car, you see mountains in the distance and herds of cattle speed by because you're clocking 70 miles an hour. The sights come so swiftly they tend to cannibalize each other. But from the seat of a bicycle, the sights and sounds of the west, the immensity and marvel of it and the random uneasiness it generates in storm make it acutely personal. From a car you are a spectator. By bicycle you are part of the action, riding in the wind or immersed in the stillness. To the west, ridge piled on ridge, and would culminate in the summits of the Wind Rivers and Grand Tetons. Amy had been there before, when we hiked to Lake Solitude in the Teton National Park, and a few years later camped in the Alaska Basin with its pageants of wild flowers; and another year when, with her younger sister, Meagan, we dodged some runaway horses that broke away from the wrangler on the trail from Death Canyon.

Amy asked me to stop, and we rolled slowly into a turnoff. She stared into the west and to the snowfields of the Wind Rivers.

"Dad," she said, "isn't this something?" Meaning, in part, isn't it great that we're doing this?

It was. There was time on this last day for that kind reverie during the five and ten minute rests we took along the highway to the Togwotee Pass beyond Dubois, which was our last overnight before we would reach the Tetons. We tented some nights, moteled the others. Now, after rest, it was time to move again and we resumed the relentless uphill grade to Togwotee, higher and higher with each turn of the road. The steepest section of the ride, thousands of feet in elevation out of Dubois, was behind us. In the little rear view mirror on my bicycle's handlebar, I searched for movement behind me near the top of one more winding hill.

In a moment my daughter's helmet bobbed around a grove of lodgepole pine, and she pumped laboriously up the pebbled asphalt to join me. Sweat bubbles jelled under her eyes, and her helmet was askew. She had to blow some vagrant hair out of her eyes.

"Less than a mile to the top of the pass," I said.

It was a promise, but it may not have registered on Amy. She puffed and swallowed, and put her foot back into the pedal stirrup. We had gained 5,000 vertical feet since leaving Riverton, Wyoming, two days before, and nearly 9,000 since we left Minneapolis—and none of it was climbed on promises.

We rolled on. The highway dipped insignificantly before the next small brow, but there was something unusual about the behavior of the small creek romping down the slope below it. It was flowing west.

"We've crossed the Continental Divide," I said over my shoulder.

Bobbing and puffing behind me, nothing more.

We stopped. And here beside the road shoulder was a sign.

"Togwotee Pass, 9,658 feet."

We had no more mountains to climb or rivers to cross. We hugged. Congratulations, stubborn young lady. She smiled wearily and then scowled. These were the 1980s. To a woman of 21 being described as a "young lady" was an affront, a moldy relic of an old and discredited sexism.

I corrected myself, remembering a furious argument we'd had a year before about the connotation of the word lady when applied to a woman.

Congratulations, young woman.

She smiled again and squeezed me. At 21, the balanced woman of the 80s was mature enough to forgive.

We had not reached the Tetons yet. They were still concealed by the inter-vening ridges. A tourist from Keokuk, Iowa, stopped his house trailer and vol-unteered to take our picture, and for five minutes we explored the blood lines and histories of the Togwotee travelers, etched on the sign. The westerners call it Toe'-gah-tee. The Crow, Shoshone and Blackfoot Indians crossed here. An Indian guide named Togwotee the Lance Thrower led a white man's expedition through. And this is where the waters divide. To the east they run to the Missouri and Wind rivers, to the west, the Snake and Columbia.

We sat for awhile, reflecting. I found myself wistful about the approaching end of our small odyssey, for all of the aches and head winds of it. The young woman had been a partner and a companion, and a rather unforgettable one. She had been someone to play road games with and someone to haggle with, and two or three times someone to cry with. But she was also someone to rely on without hesitation.

She had been ailing much of the time. We tried Bromo-Seltzer, Alka-Seltzer and most of the other remedies, plus the maiden aunt's. Still, she pedaled and enjoyed and insisted on veto power over the route we took and the cowboy cafes where we ate. We had battled for days over her contact lenses. She claimed that dust and sweat had been fouling them, so she rode without them, effectively blotting out the prairie monotony en route.

"The object on your left," I said near Lusk, Wyoming, "is a horse. I tell you that because you might have missed it."

This whistling dart failed to budge her on her bicycle seat. "I don't have to know the color of his eyes to know it's a horse," she said.

"I don't think you should use the sink water for drinking," a young body-and-fender man said in Aurora Center, S. D. "But I'll be glad to run to my grandma's to fill your bottles."

His grandmother lived nearly a quarter of a mile away. A few hours later when we stopped for information at another farm house, the folks asked us in for lunch and talk. They seemed genuinely sorry when we left. A child in the family gave us a flower, which we preserved, raggedly, for days. It was not hard to blend into this world. South of Stickney, South Dakota, we were adopted by a herd of 30 dairy cows on their way to pasture. For their route, they chose the highway, the full width of it. With no practical alternative, we joined them and continued this odd association until one of the cows lifted her tail and splattered the road in front of us with the well-known material. We fell back prudently.

During a few idling moments—all right, more than a few—I dabbled in what today we call the replay mode. A mile above sea level and 800 miles from home, we are riding the Wyoming Plateau and jousting with rattlesnakes, tumbleweed, and oil pumps. There is nothing in the footnotes of the bicycle manual advising you how to deal with terrain features like these. Maybe we should be grateful. The sauce of traveling is its surprises, and you can't pedal the American West by bicycle with any serious claim to boredom, unless you find rattlers tedious.

He was loafing on the shoulder of the road somewhere near Hell's Half Acre. I thought he was a strip of shredded tire until I saw the stripes, and at this point I executed a piece of acrobatics that defied the design engineering of my old Mariushi bicycle. The rattler must have been impressed because he swished into the field grass.

Can you imagine trying to collect a warranty, claiming your front tire was punctured by a rattlesnake?

The motorist entering the West rarely entertains thoughts like that, which is one of the bonuses of witnessing it from a bicycle seat. At that stage we were three days from the Teton Mountains. We were aching some, but feeling a rising excitement and also a kind of vulnerability that is suspenseful itself in the presence of such mighty forces. The sights and sounds of the West, the immensity and the marvel of it, and the random fright it can generate in a storm seemed more acutely personal.

You also have to dodge the odd clump of bumptious tumbleweed. I thought I had it outmaneuvered as it bounced across the highway east of Casper. But my daughter Amy was giggling behind me.

"You better stop," she said. "The tumbleweed is all snagged up in your spokes." I found no damage. How could anything as mischievous as a tumbleweed harm a stranger, here where no one speaks discouraging words.

Well, almost no one. One joy of biking through the big country is the chance to monitor the voice of America. Here's a bitching session in the Snack Shop at Crawford, Nebraska. An old farmer with 58 harvests behind him: "Three inches of rain all summer," he said. "To hell with it." But he brought in the first load of wheat—something about 12 percent moisture—and it led off the news on the Chadron radio station. His pal at the table was grousing about cars. "Why the hell did they ever stop making the Model A? It had iron on it. It gave you 22 miles a gallon. You could use bacon rind for bearings and it lasted forever. You back into a curb wrong with a new car and they cancel your insurance."

America talking. But the wanderer notices something missing.

For years the blocking dummies for this kind of talk were the bureaucrats in Washington. Out here, in the summer of 1981, they don't bitch about the federal government—at least not today. Maybe it was the Zodiac. It wasn't bad karma. In the ranch country you don't hear much talk about karma.

But now the mountains. We are riding the alkaline steppes of the great plateau. Baked and treeless, but not quite a desert. Cattle and horses and sagebrush. You can't bicycle across country like this without getting adept at fantasy. Today the winds were benign on the 104-mile leg from the antelope hunters' rendezvous at Lusk to Casper. You could Imagine that you were riding the purple sage, a cowboy chasing a stray, a ghost rider chasing his sins. Zane Grey or Frankie Laine. So why not sing? I did. "Goodbye, old paint, I'm leavin' today." The white-faced cow glared at me and mooed.

I accepted the rebuke without a grudge. Cows have rights, too.

Amy giggled again. She'd heard something on the radio. "It's a commercial for the town mortuary. They are putting on the hymn of the day." And thus, while a chorus of 55 fills the western sky with "Holy, Holy, Holy," we snort up a thousand foot hill that lifts us onto the plateau.

We must have been a sight. I had that feeling as relays of semitrailers gave us two amiable bonks on their air horns. And then I remembered that in the afternoon heat Amy had stripped down to her swimsuit top. The ultimate salute was a light blast from a passing freight train.

Never minimize the fraternity of the road.

On second thought, we were a sight. Towels and shirts never dry after the night's sudsing. So we hung them out on the bicycles' rear racks and we crossed the better part of the West like a rolling Laundromat.

The first oil field appeared east of Casper, Wyoming, announced by the mechanical mynah birds silently pumping the earth for its treasure thousands of feet below. And suddenly the New West accosted the visitor with refineries and storage tanks, Texaco and Continental conversion plants, honky-tonk music and billions in wealth.

Zane Grey, rest in peace. It's progress, unavoidable. Tumultuous. But there was no argument from me. Refineries were necessary. Jobs. Also, somewhere in the future, we were going to need some sanity not apparent then about finding better ways to get from A to B and to heat our houses. We entered Casper depressed because one private campground looked like a junkyard and another was halfway to San Francisco. A policewoman said there is a nice Lutheran minister and his wife named Holm who might be from Minneapolis. We found their home. Steve and Marilyn Holm told us there was pizza in the oven and a stretch of lawn behind their house. He had attended Northwestern Seminary in Saint Paul and she'd graduated from Augsburg College in Minneapolis We talked for hours. They were delightful and howled over the "Holy, Holy, Holy" story.

But back on the road to the Tetons, the road's shoulder was a scavenger's playground. We slalomed through the flotsam of the traveling public. In those years you could construct a whole scenario from what you saw. Here was a roll of stereo tape, two empty boxes of film and what seemed to be a used condom.

No harm there. None of that could puncture tires.

The rational mind will tell you that Hell's Half Acre, a moon crater unaccountably transported to the high semi-desert in central Wyoming, is only a geological freak. It is not supposed to produce whammies or influence the behavior of bicycles or of people who ride them. But my experience leads me to a different conclusion. I can only record three events that happened within a few miles of Hell's Half Acre.

First there was the rattler that seemed absolutely secure in its natural habitat. It had the open field advantage, nothing to worry about. But a few minutes later I spilled for the first time in a thousand miles, burying my nose in fresh blacktop while the bicycle plowed into a ditch of sagebrush.

A few miles later Amy blew her rear tire, again, for the fifth time in six days. She did it imaginatively. She did not run over a broken beer bottle or an abandoned razor blade. She flattened her tire on an office staple. I can't explain how this object came to be lying on the shoulder of one of the loneliest highways in America. But there it was in the prongs of my first aid tweezers when I examined the tube.

The replacement tube in my daughter's rear tire developed a slow leak and had to be reinflated repeatedly for the next 40 miles in places beyond the reach of surveyors and missionaries alike.

As I pumped the tire, my daughter struggled to hold some middle ground between looking grateful and laughing out loud.

As I rode, I learned more about my paradoxical young daughter, an experience that became a continuing windfall of the trip. Although she was considerate most of the time, she had no patience for what she called my Ostrich Syndrome as a traveler. Short of storm forecasts, I try to shun so-called trail information volunteered by locals or other trekkers. It's often unreliable, and I prefer discovery. I don't want to know about the length of a hill or the smell of a stagnant pond 15 miles way. There is time enough to find it.

Amy was furious with this attitude and armed herself in advance with all the technology, local prophecies and miscellaneous road chatter. "How can you NOT be prepared?" she demanded, with the autocracy of an Ivy League junior.

The young woman was willful, alert and armed with a 21-year-old's quick judgment, but also with resilience. She offered no complaint while riding 12 hours in the prairie sun but wailed about the lousy carpentry of an outhouse in a little town in South Dakota. She was a relentless goal-setter and welcomed hills because they stimulated her adrenaline. But she complained bitterly about getting up in the morning. She knew me much too well to attribute elaborate nobility to the good things I do or malice to the bad. While she crabbed or razzed here and there, she would sometimes see my preoccupation with another part of my life, and there was tenderness in how she edged into my thoughts. She accepted sprains, sunburn and high wind but worried nearly to death about looking ragged riding to town.

She was one man's daughter, and the more I thought about it, the less joy I found in the approaching end of the ride.

We didn't always identify where we were going in our rambling talks in camp at night. One night we reminisced about her mother, Rose, my former wife. I apologized and accepted blame for the divorce that altered Amy's life and that of her sister, Meagan, in their adolescence. Those times in our lives did not dominate our talk, but they were on the edges. By opening my eyes to her growth from the child and school girl I remembered to the vibrant and confident woman she'd become, I found a recreational ride in the mountains turning into a watershed in my life.

It was hard to respond as candidly as she insisted when the talk moved to my periodic drinking. It was also impossible to predict then that 12 years later hers would be the most compelling single voice turning me in the direction of the recovery I enjoy today. Remembering our trip now—

through the prisms of her subsequent career, her marriage and motherhood two years afterward, and my life of health and sobriety today—fills me with an appreciation that will last a lifetime.

Still, there wasn't all that much solemnity. We were traveling together, 24 hours a day, pedaling, sweating, gawking, waving at folks, feuding and singing and sucking up the sunlight of a new day and the most marvelous scenery in America. The day was free and the sky was the limit. I felt something else, the electricity of exerting physically in a big world of high horizons, miles of prairie, mountains beyond it and the open road. The west wind always excited me. But today it seemed generous, not much more than a breeze, and we were nearing the high mountains.

How are you going to overdo solemnity when the cows are taunting you, the transistor radio is bringing you gossip from the Sand Hills and a dog wants to jump into your tent? But when my friends ask about it now, I tell them it was a time and the kind of journey I would urge on others. In today's society of lightning change in culture and relationships, there is only a narrow window when parents and children reach a point in age when they can freely act and talk together as adults, and together explore the road and their lives. They might, I add, discover someone a little different from what they expected.

They might also discover Togwotee Pass.

Our rest at Togwotee ended with the onset of storm clouds. We were now traveling downhill, but we did no exuberant leaping from ridge to ridge. The bicycle is a fragile machine. These are powerful mountains. The road dives thousands of feet and forgives no runaways. It was also wet. So we nursed the bicycles mile after mile, surrendering the downhill euphoria to higher demands of self-preservation.

And then the Tetons erupted before us through a clearing in the trees. Did it matter that they have presented that stunning scene dozens of time? Did it matter that the orchestration of snow and granite were so familiar to us that we could identify every summit, and sense the trail dust in the canyons miles away?

They never lose their spontaneity and their drama or their power to churn the blood. They sweep straight out of the valley in cliffs thousands of feet high, creating peaks stark and virile, competing with each other for the onlooker's wonder.

I first came to the valley of Jackson Hole in the 1950s. The architects and bulldozers have moved the buildings and changed the roads and pulled out most of the commerce from the national park, and there is still peace and restoration here. There is excitement if you want it. It is the essence of the national park idea, the ultimate proof that not all of the land must be thrown to the machines to feed the gullet of progress and the gross national product. No gold or uranium is extracted here. Yet it has enlarged the lives of millions of people. It has turned their directions, permitted them to relocate themselves with nature and to rediscover their earth. You can come to these mountains as hiker, climber, wildflower ogler, as tourist or bicyclist. The Grand Tetons are an ideal, a statement of a powerful and exquisitely wild nature, at the service of the communicant. If you are seeking that ideal, there are places and seasons where you will usually find it here.

One last puzzlement overtook my daughter.

"Dad, you must have taken that picture two dozen times over the years."

It wasn't a reprimand. She did wonder if there is any conceivable new angle for a picture of Mount Moran from the Oxbow Bend of the Snake River. The camera might have agreed, because it was out of film.

"Tommy Tourist strikes out," she mourned.

We had come all that distance, and learned so much. We found deeper worth not only in each other, I think, but in the benevolence of the land we traveled and the people who came into our lives.

We slept well on the shore of Jackson Lake that night, with no more wheels to turn.

Dorothy, Jerri, and Linda:
Lives Joined by the Northern Stars

I will wait my appointment each September until another moment when I, too, perhaps shall appear in a new time, in another season ... to love again.

—Jerri Kyle

No one I've encountered in my travels has been able to tell me whether Dorothy Molter, Jerri Kyle, and Linda Phillips met. It would make sense if they had.

Dorothy Molter and Jerri Kyle were women of the Minnesota north country. It became the lodestone of their lives, their provider and their sanctuary. The north was in their blood. It gave them their strength and comfort and spirituality. Dorothy Molter was a durable and maternal custodian of the snows. For six months through the long winter she lived in isolation on an island in Minnesota's Boundary Waters. She was temperamentally suited to understand the winter's severities and its hours of splendor.

Jerri Kyle came to the north with the wounds of a childhood illness but no disposition to be intimidated by them. She was a whirlwind in the wheelchair she needed for mobility, a woman charged with energy and creativity, sketching lighthouses and gulls, pondering the afterlife, and writing hymns to the surf of Lake Superior.

Linda Phillips was a beautiful woman disabled by an automobile accident that broke her back and ended her marriage. The trauma might have marked her as a victim for the rest of her life. Instead, it created a tiger insisting on freedom. In later years, as her strength waned and her immobility deepened, life for Linda became something close to a daily combat to wring something of value from her diminishing years—a service to contribute, a right to assert or a rainbow to find. It also became a personal campaign to unite herself with the winds and sunrises and a glistening waters of the northland she revered.

All three of them are gone now. But in my remembrances they are forever linked with the mystiques and the indefinable power the north country exerts on those whose longings and aura need it—the space, the silence, the uncorrupted starlight and the raw might of the wilderness. What made them alike was a quality they stamped on their lives and personalities, a need to discover an ultimate fulfillment despite their vulnerabilities and the improbable settings of those lives.

Dorothy Molter's rhythms were quieter and rarely burdened despite her solitary life. She lived alone on an island in Knife Lake—one of three that were connected by tiny bridges—not far from the Canadian border. There she became a friend and by mutual agreement a kind of godmother to canoeists in summer, and to the less congested numbers of skiers, snowshoers, and snowmobilers in the winter.

She was the daughter of an itinerant railroad man who introduced her to the Minnesota's north woods nearly sixty years ago. As a trained nurse, she gave care to a retired logger who owned the islands then. When he died, he bequeathed her the islands and cabins. She made an annual trip to Chicago for years to renew her nurse's license, but in time settled in to become, with the death of Bennie Ambrose a few lakes over, the last year-round inhabitant of the Boundary Waters canoe country. Federal law threatened to evict them both in the mid-1970s. But the government yielded to the cries of their friends and admirers, and to common sense. The government said they could stay as long as they lived, which they did.

Eventually Dorothy acquired the status of a kind of wilderness celebrity and, after her death, a growing legend.

I met her several times. Thousands did. On my first visit I left a winter camp on a ski trip with a friend and called on her at her cottage. She had become an institution by then. But both on that day and on subsequent visits I saw nothing that suggested a woman privately enjoying or basking in celebrity. What I saw was a person such as I'd rarely met, let alone one living in seclusion—someone who seemed so completely at peace with life and the world.

We spent an hour in conversation and it was one to engrave. She talked about her kinship with the animals, her life as a nurse and then as a kind of matronly landmark, and the stacks of Christmas cards she wrote by the hour. She spoke of the friendships she rekindled around her platters of cookies, the winter, her memories, and the times the wolf packs would assemble on the ice a few feet from her cottage.

She had a gun that she never used. She understood the wolves, and it seemed to be mutual. Wolves aren't dumb, especially in the winter. Where humans live, there are bound to be scraps of food and bones to gnaw. Dorothy understood that the wolves of northern Minnesota were big enough and tough enough to find their own food in the woods. But they sometimes found the odd leftover around Dorothy's cabin. Not often. Dorothy Molter didn't spend decades in the wild country without learning that it's not smart to coddle wolves.

She was not a hermit. She was a woman comfortable with the winter and her isolation from the baubles of the workaday world. Her response to the luxuries of life—clothes, entertainment, travel, diversity—was pure Dorothy. "Some people need those. And I say, 'enjoy them. You've earned them.' But all I have is here on the island. I go into town (Ely) when I need to or want to. But otherwise this is my life. I never get lonely. I can hear music and the news. But I told myself a long time ago, 'What I have is priceless to me.'"

In the December of northern Minnesota winters, the sun is a pale orange tease. By 5 o'clock it basically disappears; by 4:30 if you were Dorothy Molter and lived a few miles south of the Canadian border. It actually wasn't deserting Dorothy. The earth and the wind and stars and even the sun seemed to have an affinity for her.

Our talk never threatened the borders of profundity, but here was a woman, living alone through the northern winter, who was a pleasant and convivial hostess, smiling often, offering pastries, inquiring about the other's life and travels, behaving nothing like the recluse that one might have expected.

It was near Christmas, a coincidence, because a few hundred miles away millions of people were trying rather desperately to achieve the kind of serenity and thanksgiving that was there so simply in the face of Dorothy Molter.

The brief fulfillment that the rest of us feel during the holidays may last only a few hours before it gets pretty well ground up by reality. People fight, bills arrive, and the telephone goes nuts. Still, we know in our hearts that those few hours of shared magnanimity in the world are worth it, and for that reason there's nothing wrong with imagining a life where there is true internal calm. Such a life doesn't have to be a saint's, and it was Dorothy Molter's.

In fact, it was Dorothy Molter's especially at Christmas time because there were Christmas nights in her life when she sat staring at the northern lights, alone on her island in the pines, silently startled by the glory of it.

Dorothy was a person of ordinary virtues who created an extraordinary life by discovering herself, being content with what she found, and understanding both her horizons and her limits. Relationships were good, but she did not have to be dependent on them. There are some kinds of love that do not require passion, some kinds of peace that do not need evangelism.

She struck me as a person who seldom looked for any dramatic definition or symbolism in her solitary life in the north woods. She was civil and pleasant as a conversationalist, never pretending that she was some kind of reborn Bird Woman facing a frontier. As the mistress of her little islands for 56 years, she was a collector and a putterer. She grew things and collected recipes, ornaments, letters, and the names of thousands of canoeists who dropped in to chat. She lived privately for months, but she was not a recluse. Her limits were her fundamental needs: a kinship with the earth, her understanding of her place in it, and an appreciation of both the earth and the people who passed through her life.

She never looked on her island life as an escape. It was a union of her spirit with the winds of autumn, the wolf's call, the solemnities of winter, and the eagerness of spring. In her later years she had a kind of stolid physique and chubby face that cloaked her femininity. Her psychological toughness and stubbornness did not conflict with the poetry she felt when the sun burst over the lake and renewed her.

She read her books and wrote her letters, and once in a while she strapped on her snowshoes and trudged for hours on the frozen lakes to reach the town of Ely. Sometimes she would be awakened by a wolves' chorale on the ice a few hundred feet from her cabin. When snowmobiles came, it was easier to keep her pantry stocked and more fun, too, because she genuinely enjoyed the yarn-telling and the small talk. And she knew, without smugness, that the respect her he-man visitors felt for her was real. But when the visitors were gone, she became the custodian of her island again, tuned to the sounds of the lake and forest. "One of the sounds I've always liked best is the water in summer," she said. "We don't have huge waves here. But you can go down to the water when the sun has been up for an hour or so and things are warm, and birds are calling and feeding, and the water along the shore just seems to be telling you that the world is OK, and you don't need much more than this." That is the poetry of a hardy and a very perceptive woman.

"I think what I like best about living alone up here is the quiet," she said. "I also like the different attitudes you get from the change in season. The spring is best. The woods come alive again. The summer is busy and beautiful. The fall makes you think and the winters make you struggle a little. But to see the flowers and the birds and leaves again, that makes it all worth it. I do love it. Sometimes people ask if this is a life for a woman. I have to say, why not a woman?"

Dorothy shared a confidence. "Right now, I'm dieting. One meal a day for Dorothy." She wasn't so sure about the wolves. "I saw the strangest thing not long ago," she said. "I heard something about ten in the morning and went outside the porch. There they were, lined up together, right near my water hole, twelve wolves. They were doing a little yelping but not much. I don't think I was scared. They didn't seem too interested in me. I went back into the cabin for a minute, and when I came out they were walking slowly across the lake, single file."

And Dorothy watched them go, holding not a rifle but a camera.

She died at seventy-nine in her log cabin in December 1986. It was a few days before a Christmas she would have observed with her angels' hair and her search of the sky for the aurora borealis, which always told her this was the northern night, and all in the world was well.

The world might not allow many more Dorothy Molters. But what she was saying was that if you bring to the world limits you can understand and appreciate, peace might follow. She found it on an island. The rest of us may not be so venturesome or lucky, but she'd say it's there if you look.

I'd guess that Dorothy and Jerri Kyle would have talked for hours if the stars actually had brought them together. Jerri Kyle lived alone for years in her cottage on the shore of Lake Superior a few miles north of the town of Two Harbors. It was not the same kind of solitary life as Dorothy's, but it undoubtedly was harder. Because of polio in her childhood she needed a wheelchair to navigate her home, to get into her car, to follow a path to the great inland sea where she would sit enthralled beside her 150 feet of lakefront and spend hours there watching and listening to the surf, sketching, writing poems to it, and feeling the spray.

I knew her for better than ten years, and never heard a sound of resentment or any kind of moping sadness. She was sometimes distracted by the awkwardness of getting around, although never embarrassed by it. More often she imagined herself flying down the North Shore on a bicycle or chasing butterflies in the thickets between her cottage and the highway. She sometimes had fun pretending to be impatient with her clumsiness getting from here to there. My regret now is that because we knew each other only casually I too often accepted the surface Jerri Kyle, with her effervescent salutes to the day and to life. If I'd known her better I would have risked her disapproval by exploring her pain and the might-have-beens of her life.

She was one of those uncommon people that the newspaper columnist will meet in his daily wanderings and noodlings. Just as often some of those uncommon people will come into his office because they have something to say. Jerri wheeled herself into my office. She was convinced she had psychic powers, and for all I know she did. I spent about five minutes considering her psychic powers but I was more genuinely drawn to her poetry and her sketches, and her vibrancy despite the wheelchair. She laughed incessantly, a few times at my innocence about the great and murky psychic world.

But she was serious about her art, and she valued the prizes she won. And then she began talking about Lake Superior, and the psychic world quickly disappeared from my field of curiosity.

Lake Superior was the ocean of my own childhood. It has fostered hundreds of interpreters and artists, but none, it seemed to me, who had done it more lovingly and with a personal commitment so powerful and urgent as Jerri Kyle's. Other artists were more skillful. With Jerri, the lake seemed to be close to life itself. I asked her to tell me about it. On some mornings, she said, the sun rising over the lake all but burst through the windows of the porch where she slept, and the swish of the surf against the rocks seemed to turn time around. For many years she needed no other geography in her life. There was the great water and the orange globe leaping out of it to spread its warmth. This and Jerri Kyle. Nothing more.

She'd awake, toss off the covers, and wriggle and grunt into her wheelchair to get the coffee going in the kitchen. The world now being in order, she'd trundle back into her porch.

The Superior sea, she believed, had inexplicable powers to transform time. She was sure of that. At some hours this place was her Oz. Freaky figures arrayed themselves outside her window, sculpted by the sea spray in winter or by the wind savaging the tree limbs in the fall. Other nights it was her safe haven, not from the rudeness of the world but from her temptations to be soured by it. Her Tinkertoy cabin by the lake was never an escape. She didn't need flight. What she needed were the cries of the gulls. She needed the sun's rays drying out the ancient red slab rock that had been laundered for centuries by the lake. When the sun did that, the earth and Jerri Kyle were cleansed.

Although it seemed to shift identities on a whim, her porch reverted to a workaday role about 9 a.m. each day. It was her studio. One day she'd paint a gull landing on a roosting rock in the bay. The next day she might write a poem about the unlimited dreams of a turtle.

And then one summer, her Oz was gone. After six years she sold her cottage to take an apartment overlooking a suburban shopping center outside of Duluth, a place not famous for transforming time.

I asked her why. How could she abandon the spray of the big breakers and the squawking gulls for a suburban apartment? Was it money, loneliness, what? If it was money, why not sell the old cement mixer she'd squirreled away?

"It's none of that," she said. "The winters never get lonely, but they do get to be a hassle for one person trying to keep up the place." She didn't say one woman, or one disabled woman struck by polio when she was ten. She made her acceptances years ago, first when she lost the use of her legs, and later when she lost her marriage through divorce not long after she and her husband moved into the cottage a few miles north of Two Harbors.

Some time before that she found out she could paint well enough to sell. After a few more years she made the same discovery about poetry, which may be harder to sell than old plastic. She wrote about the sunrise and fields of flax and about dreams and foolishness. Pretty standard fare. But she had a feel for reverie without drenching it in emotionalism.

Conversationally, she giggled and spewed out putdowns of her labors and her solitary life. But in the few times I visited I never had trouble figuring out that this was posturing, her way of being sociable. She didn't want to make something profound out of living alone by the big lake in the north woods. She did the same with her spiritual life, which was a rather chaotic mixture of conventional religion with random plunges into the beyond of extra-sensory perception and messaging. She didn't call it spiritualism. But from the time her mother died she found herself treading on the edges of a spirit world. She was convinced that there were times when she was being guided to draw this or to write that. She idealized nature and human relationships, searching for tenderness in how we treat nature, how nature treats us, and how we treat each other. Privately, she sometimes spoofed the intensity of that search. Jerri and her muse. She laughed often, and it enhanced the attractiveness of her strong and animated face. When she giggled she did it in trills and arpeggios, as though trying to find music in the delight she felt at the moment. She experienced that often in her first years of solitude by the lake. Winter was a gift of God rather than a penance for life in Minnesota. The frozen water pipes and high snowdrifts she had to deal with were somewhat less impressive gifts. She pretended to grumble about those and about her predicaments getting in and out of the wheelchair. But she was amazingly adroit at it.

Life in the winter for a disabled woman, though, even one with the will and the creativity of Jerri Kyle, became burdensome. She decided all this was taking her into the life of a recluse. She enjoyed human chatter too much for that. She liked to talk poetry and art with other members of a tiny arts society that gave her energy. So she sold her cottage and moved to an apartment on the headland above Duluth. The groceries were easier to fetch. There were more voices to mix with, and long talks about free verse lubricated with a few cans of beer.

Then, as before, her disability seemed rarely to absorb her. She called September the season of her soul, and in September I bought a little sketch she drew of Split Rock Lighthouse encircled by gulls. It was done with grace and insight and must be worth five times what I paid for it. Since we'd been friends for years, she refused to take more.

Of the sketch she wrote, "I will wait my appointment each September until another moment when I, too, perhaps shall appear in a new time, in another season ... to love again."

She wrote and sketched at her new home with as much zeal as before, and died a few years later, not far from Lake Superior, and still within sight of it. I think in the end the psychic longings she nurtured most of her life may have buoyed her and intensified as she approached death, and she was earnestly attracted to the idea of appearing "in a new time, to love again."

And she may.

Linda Phillips, tragically disabled on her honeymoon, could only hunger for those moments she had idealized—the sun rays flowing through a pine forest and the swishing of a stream beside her tent. She imagined herself soaking in those sensations: Linda alone in the woods. Except for two or three brief reprieves from the deterioration of her body, she could only imagine experiencing the north country as Dorothy Molter and Jerri Kyle did. She struggled all of her adult life to squeeze in some of those moments. She fought from a wheel chair and later inert from a bed in the public housing high rise apartment in Minneapolis where she spent her final years. She read John Muir to embrace the mountains and woods. Sometimes she seethed. The gifts of the woods were available to the casual stroller but were denied to her, who needed them so desperately. It was stifling, unfair and monstrous, she thought, the cruelest of all conditions for a woman who wanted and needed involvement with her world. And yet she found a way before life ended at the age of 50.

The lady slipper of the north's brief summer is a kind of wild orchid, lovely and fragile and intricate, but oddly tough. It was, and also is, Linda. The present tense is preferred. I can explain why. Most of her life was pain and busted visions and scrabbling years of coping in a wheelchair, that and her undefeatability. It was the kind of life not bound by markers of time or even death.

She was the human spirit pounded by blows of grotesque unfairness. But like a wildflower growing out of scorched earth, she was somehow adaptable to them and even forgiving of them. She was a gorgeous bride with long black hair and a limitless future. She had brains and guts and looks and ambition. She could have reigned over society galas or stood in a protest line and stared down polluters. She could have run for Congress or kicked the butt of a seal hunter. She was that strong and that motivated.

And then their car plunged over a cliff on their honeymoon in Mexico, and the world became a horror. It did for a time. All right, the world was never very kind for Linda after her paralysis. Why should this woman of so much energy and wit and with so many dragons to fight have to be hobbled with dependency? Why was it Linda who would never have children and never experience a day without pain or a day without some lingering symptoms of the might-have-beens?

Why should somebody who heard music in the woods and in the middle of a storm, go deaf? She did ask those questions. Eventually, she came to terms. Others, she said, had it worse. She still had choices. She couldn't run a marathon, but she didn't have to give up being Linda Phillips. If she were still going to be Linda Phillips and stay sane, she had to resist the poison of resentment and martyrdom. Being cantankerous all the time was deadly. Being cantankerous part of the time, when she had a cause to fight, could be productive.

She was never quite sure whether she could make a difference. I know she did and how she did and why the falling ashes of Linda Phillips' should have meant something to all of us that weekend after she died.

Linda and her husband were divorced several years after the accident. There were no excessively hard feelings. Their lives had changed. Each of them carried a separate kind of grief and altered goals. Hers were to revere the earth and living things and to keep her mind restless and honed. Her immobility first stung her. If you want the truth, it enraged her. God, what are you doing? Then she decided on a wily strategy. She would outwit and outlast her paralysis.

When the airlines refused to let her ride in a wheelchair years ago, she campaigned against them with speeches and ridicule. When that failed, she tried mischievous poems and charm, and she was as good at that as she was with her harpoons. So she flew. When they said it would be hard for her to ride in a canoe, she found somebody, Wilderness Inquiry, to say it could be done. "We can't go through our ritual of dunking you as a beginner," they said. "Dunk me," she said. They did. She spluttered to the surface, laughing. Wasn't this the most glorious day of her life? she asked. It was, until she slept under the Northern Lights and saw a bear and heard the hail on her tent roof in a thunderstorm. Then that became the most glorious day. Storms thrilled her. The electricity in them seemed to restore her inert muscles and charge her emotions, and she would regret it when the storm died.

We met eight or nine times. She enlisted me as a co-conspirator, first in her campaign to shame the airlines and later to find a way to get her to Africa. She asked if it was OK if she considered me a brother. I said I'd be honored to be a relative as long as it wasn't an uncle or grandfather. We exchanged secrets. She wanted to know how she could help save this or that. She needed public assistance to live in her apartment. She had no money, which didn't mean she couldn't make donations. She found two dollars for Save the Whales. She gave three dollars a year for retarded kids, usually with a poem. She tried to save trees and rhinos, and if there had been a fund to save anteaters, she would have given to that. If it breathed or if it streaked sap, it was kin for Linda. She wrote and read, and once in a while she would stare at the ceiling from her bed and say, when nobody heard, "Am I really making it?"

I don't think she knew how much she made it. At her funeral service, scores of folks gave testimony. They wept and giggled. They loved her values and respected how she refused to withdraw. They found her wrath hilarious, and her pensive moods divine. Someone said this: "Imagine a person having shrunk to eighty pounds, and dealing daily with pain, being so lyrical to imagine herself in the middle of a flower, feeling its colors change?"

Linda never stopped exploring. She was one of the purest adventurers I've ever met. She made a demand on me one day. "Tell me what you feel in the Himalayas." I said I feel what's expressed when the Nepalese greet each other and say "Namaste."

"Show me how it is pronounced on this pad," she said. "Nahmah-stay," I wrote. "It means what?" "It means 'I praise the god who lives within you.'"

With her hand, she asked me to come closer. She wasn't crying, but her eyes were misted "Do you believe that?" she asked. Believe what? "That something immortal and good lives in us?" I said I do. She smiled. I think it was in agreement. And I think she knew more than I did.

She died with the request that her ashes should be cast in springtime into the woods and water and winds of the Boundary Waters where, she said, she once met a lady slipper. That is romantic and good. But what Linda brought to the northern woods near Seagull Lake that day, and thereafter, doesn't have to meet the theologian's definition of immortality. What Linda left that is more important is the strength of her struggle and her refusal to give up her humanity. It makes a wildflower something special.

10

A Reunion Beneath the Matterhorn

On Christmas Eve in 2006, nearly 50 years after we first climbed the Matterhorn together, Gottlieb Perren walked into a small hotel in the Swiss village of Zermatt beneath the mountain. The hour that followed became a reenactment of a part of my life that would not have been the same without him.

We shook hands near a window from where, in the approaching twilight, you could see the Matterhorn filling the sky through the tossing snowflakes.

"*Gruss Gott,*" I said.

He smiled, pretending to be impressed by the quality of my clumsy German. He wore a vividly patterned blue and white ski sweater over shoulders that looked square and sturdy after all the years. He was 80 years old, still athletic despite the slight limp from a skiing accident on a glacier early in his mountaineering life. His strong physical appearance surprised me. He might just as well have carried a coiled climbing rope into the hotel. His face had lost none of the taut virility of the postered Swiss mountain guide. He was a Bergfuhrer still, although no longer climbing.

He was more talkative than the tightly focused guide of our climbing years, even courtly. Between words he seemed to be saying what his careful Swiss reserve could not quite tell me directly, "It's good to be together again."

We talked easily for an hour about our climbs on the Matterhorn, the Obergabelhorn, the Wellenkuppe and more. For a while his face grew absolutely elfin. "You know," he said, "sometimes you were a little crazy."

(Left) The Matterhorn of the Swiss Alps is everlastingly alluring to hikers, climbers and photographers. It is the ultimate in mountains—the mountain a child imagines mountains to be.

I think he might have used some elliptical form of *dumkopf.* "We came down that long ridge on the Obergabelhorn, the Arbengrat, and when we got down from the rock to the snow you made this long jump. And I couldn't believe it. That was the *bergschrund*, where the snow and ice pull away from the mountain. I thought you were gone. The worst part—we were still roped. We both would have gone!"

I told him I still remembered The Great Bergfuhrer's shriek of disapproval. But I felt oddly reserved myself about asking a question that I never really asked him as he approached the end of his climbing years. I was only a few years younger. Although I still trek high in the Himalayas, I've had to admit that there are probably not going to be any more Matterhorns or Huascarans or Eigers for me.

Gottlieb Perren

I wanted to know what kind of regret he felt, now that his serious climbing days were over. Was his life somehow diminished? What part of an active life would be lost along with the excitement of one more climb in the mountains? Or was all that empty, noodling melodrama?

Yet I never asked him. And I have to tell myself today: he didn't seem very devastated to me. In the window, he jauntily raised a glass to Das Matterhorn.

A historic mountain? Oh, yes. It dominates the poetry and legends of early mountaineering. It thrusts itself in front of the gaping traveler with all the qualities that are demanded of a great mountain. It is regal, aloof and peerlessly photogenic. Some travelers seeing it for the first time call it beautiful. Others are actually scared. It may depend on what the sight of mountains does with your mind. Does it conjure mystery and foreboding, or the hand of God? Among those who climb, there is the endless fascination with the ghosts of the Matterhorn, of those who have died, most of them through foolishness or complacently.

But here was the Matterhorn, again, back in my life, and I could have stood all night at the window of the little hotel, sifting through the climbs we made, and the faces. It didn't matter that it has been climbed thousands of times. If you have never climbed, the Matterhorn remains the mountain of your imagination. It is both elegant and sinister, a great white citadel with a notorious past and an almost irresistible allure to anyone who has looped a climbing rope around his or her waist and looked up at its great summit crown.

If you'll pardon me, I WILL talk about the Matterhorn and ghosts.

I first saw it on leave from my Army post in Germany in the early 1950s. I had no intention of climbing it. I had no mountaineering training and I came gaping like a few million others who've viewed this mountain for the first time. The approach trail beneath it was easily negotiable. I walked through the groves of aromatic Arolla pines and experienced the normal excitement as the Matterhorn expanded before me until, above the tiny lake called the Schwarzee, I felt the first twitches of wonder—at its history, its massiveness so close and its imperious posture. I'd come up through the village of Zermatt, whose cemetery beside the old Catholic Church seemed a silent, maudlin indictment of the dumb recklessness of climbing mountains in the first place. The phrase "dumb recklessness" is one of those usually applied by calmer minds who like to deride the idea of climbing as a refuge for exhibitionists and the emotionally unbalanced.

Part of this charge is probably correct. But, then, there are exhibitionists on the battlefield, in the football arenas, and in the bedroom. It would be years before I'd feel any obligation to try to sort out the purists and recreationalists from the grandstanders and the death-wish fanatics on a mountain slope. Though I didn't know it then, I would eventually climb the Matterhorn eight times at intervals that pretty much marked my personal passages from young adulthood through middle age and on to the mossy gates of the septuagenarian. So this mountain, so magnetic in its demeanor and obliging to even the semi-skilled climber on ordinary days—yet so famously homicidal—became for me the Polaris of my search in the high world.

I was thirty when I climbed the Matterhorn for the first time with Gottlieb. I'd begun to climb in the Grand Tetons of western Wyoming a few years before and learned the fundamentals of rope management and climbing technique. The hotel manager gave me Gottlieb's name, we met for dinner and we agreed to the climb. I remember the guide's fee: $35. It's in the range of a $1,000 today. He gave the appearance of a serious man, Teutonic blonde, big shouldered, frugal with his talk and with no pressing need for smiles of congeniality and gemutlichkeit. He didn't change that much in the years that followed. Most climbing guides resist personal relationships with clients. There are cultural differences and long intervals between contact. The clients come and go. Some of them are terrified. Others are brash.

But we did develop a personal relationship, and when I'd call Gottlieb from Minneapolis to reserve a couple of days in summer, he was always on the brink of giving me the usual caveat about storm clouds, when I would interrupt and mimic him and say in tangled English and German, *"Ja, aber it depends on das Wetter, Mein Bergfuhrer."* It usually cracked him up and he always kept a climb open for me. I don't know if he ever realized his role in my lifelong attachment to the mountains, or his impact on my life.

Instead of taking the cable car to the Schwarzee Hotel at 9,400 feet on the approach to the Matterhorn's climber's hut, I hiked up on the trail actually used by Whymper and his party on the first ascent nearly a hundred years before. It switched back through the forest for two thousand feet and opened a vast highland of snow peaks, glaciers and dashing rivulets. I made the hike in something close to a trance. My own journey was now joined with the mountaineering demigods, Whymper, Croz, Carrell and the others. Ghosts abounded and I couldn't get enough. I relished each stride and, feeling strong and a little invincible, I practically flew up the trail to the overnight hut, where I met Gottlieb. He'd taken the cable car. Why not? He'd been here 300 times. We met for five minutes after the supper of bratwurst and rosti potatoes. The conversation was not overdosed with drama. Perren always looked on weather as some kind of latent family curse, lying in ambush. He was gruff, which under the conditions might have been a moral victory for his client. So I settled for that. "The weather is not the best," he said. "We'll be in cloud (fog). The guardian (hut manager) will get you up at 2 o'clock in the morning."

"Jawohl, Herr Bergfuhrer," I thought. I wasn't offended. The Matterhorn, the prospect of climbing it, carried too much emotional voltage for that. The small dorm rooms upstairs were furnished primitively with two-tier military cots and bore the lingering aroma of urine from the john at the end of the short hallway. I spread my pack and gear at the foot of the cot, slipped under the sheet and wool blanket and fell

into a sleep interrupted only once, around midnight, when the sounds of an avalanche down the mountain's North Face jolted me awake. Were these the ghosts, shaking their chains or their carabiners or whatever it is ghosts rattle on the Matterhorn? More likely thousands of tons of ice and snow cutting loose harmlessly out of range of the climb's hut beneath our route, the Hornli ridge. I didn't feel any foreboding about it. The Matterhorn was a mountain with all of the trappings: History, theater, architectural style, and the normal convulsions of a 14,700-foot mountain in the Alps. What the avalanche did was to stir me to the toes, a sensation that cost me a half hour of sleep but seemed to expand the adventure. What was a climb of the Matterhorn without the prelude of an avalanche in the dead of night?

The hutkeeper's knock on the door was abrupt. Despite my excitement, I had to admit it was vaguely intrusive and unsettling. There's a quirky part of the human psyche that rebels against reality horning in on fantasy. You can safely indulge fantasies lying under a wool blanket in a mountain hut. The hutkeeper's wake-up call at 2 a.m. is reality butting in. It's also the signal for some informal snarling and cursing in the dorm room because boots and sweaters suddenly are not tidily arrayed at the foot of the bunk but have fallen someplace on the darkened and scruffy floor. The guy bunking below me was scrambling around the floor looking for his climbing clothes without the guidance of his headlamp, which was useless because he'd let the batteries run down. And right about there you could scratch one potential Matterhorn summit climber, because if your personal organization is that lousy lying in a bunk it's not going to be much better climbing a 4,000 foot cliff.

I'd come without my own equipment but Gottlieb's La Cabana store conveniently provided rental for the boots and crampons at moderate prices. I joined Gottlieb for a fast mug of coffee and unbuttered rye bread. We roped up and walked the 50 yards to the cold black rock wall where the Matterhorn's northeast ridge joined the glacial moraine.

The dense fog thinned the ranks of would-be climbers quickly. While today hordes answer that 2 o'clock doorknock, only 12 did on that July day in 1958. Five of those peeled off after 10 minutes in the fog. The rest moved upward but by the time Gottlieb and I reached the emergency Solvay Hut two-thirds of the way up, we were alone on the Matterhorn.. Gottlieb asked

(Next page) Jim Klobuchar approaches the summit ridge of the Matterhorn on his eighth ascent of the mountain. Although thousands have climbed the Matterhorn over the decades—and nearly a thousand have died in the attempt—it remains the beau ideal of climbing.

me once if I'd rather go down. "If we go to the summit," he said. "You won't be able to see five feet in front of you."

I asked the *bergfuhrer* if he saw any serious danger of being benighted on the mountain, the blank visibility and all. Gottlieb's answer was no answer at all. It was simply Gottlieb in all of its opaque ambiguity. "This is a mountain," he said. "There is always danger."

Well, that's very good, Gottlieb. He looked back to me, tilted his jaw upward and threw back his head slightly, the universal gesture for: "What do you want to do?"

I grinned at him, because I was dying to go on. As unheroically as I could, I lifted my arm toward the summit, or where I thought was the summit. There were no stars, no moon. We were walking in soup and, in fact, the mountain itself, except for the part 30 yards in any direction from us, was invisible. But the way was up. The fog obliterated the normal landmarks of the route, but that couldn't have fazed Perren. These people are not famous for flights of romanticism. That never disappointed me, in Gottlieb or any of his chums. My gold stars on an alpine climb, as the bedrock requirement for a guide, went first to Competence and Judgment. My silver stars went to Competence and Judgment. Affability usually came in a distant third.

We rounded an awkward bend in the first few minutes of the climb and from Perren's head lamp picked out the steps and holds as we made our way up the easy first sections of the climb and then onto the higher-angle but still untroubled rock pitches. They lifted us some 2,000 feet to the Solvay Hut, where we rested for a few minutes. The visibility wasn't any better after dawn. We reached the snowpack and the beginning of fixed ropes. Here the ridge shot upward almost vertically, in the shadow of the north face of the mountain, the hardest of all of its routes. The fixed rope is not for hand over hand climbing. You grabbed the fixed rope with one hand, used the other to find a hold in the rock or snow, jammed your crampons into the hard-packed snow or ice, and moved upward. Every 40 or 50 feet Gottlieb stopped to reel in the belay rope that connected us, tied it into a fixed bolt in the mountain side and anchored himself while I came up. It was essentially muscle work, and my movements were competent and brisk if not lathered with grace. The exposures were terrific, 3,000 and 4,000 foot drops below our inch-deep foot and handholds, but in the fog, looking up or down pretty much presented the same view. It also dulled the climber's rarest satisfaction in reaching the summit, as we did a few minutes later. On this day there was not that inimitable charge you feel being engulfed by a stunning world of blue ice and blue sky and great whorls of meringue sweeping across the mountainscape from horizon to horizon. Today there were no mountains to see from the top of the most celebrated of mountains, including this mountain itself. The fog obliterated all. But the rest would come on another time. Gottlieb nodded in approval, said "good work, Jeem," we shared a salami sandwich, and went down.

After we reached the overnight hut I hiked down another hour and a half to the Schwarzee, where my wife Rose was waiting. I was touched and grateful for that. She could have stayed in the valley, but this was the Matterhorn and her parents were Swiss, and it seemed right to walk down together in the rain.

For me, reaching the summit of this legendary mountain was an immense reward for effort, yes, and a time for a quiet celebration of an ideal I had created for myself. The fog on top didn't reduce the gratification of it. I thought of the climb as a beginning. It was the beginning of an honest passion. I thought there were going to be years ahead of mountains and the clinking of ice axes and mysterious cliffs and the shocks of joy when the sun exploded out of the summits of the horizons.

And so there were.

You can get lost in the introspections of climbing. For a time I indulged those, when it seemed right and informative to probe motivations and needs. Was there some naked appeal simply in the risk? Well, there was risk for sure. How much? It depended on your skills and your companions and your mountain, I suppose. So what about risk? Anybody who swims the Channel or skis the slaloms or rides at Indy or surfs or scuba dives has to reach a certain level of self-indulgence, going for something not everybody feels strong enough or loopy enough to try. So what I experienced in the fog that morning was probably the fulfillment of having done something arduous and demanding without feeling electrified about it. Later, climbing settled comfortably under my skin and I avoided most of such mental acrobatics. I realized that sometimes I was going to fail. I realized that I had no special reason to feel elite standing on top of the Matterhorn when I couldn't see the top of the Matterhorn.

The Matterhorn of 1958 was part of the education. The Matterhorn of 15 years later might have been its completion. By then I knew mountaineering as well as I was going to. I'd acquired most of the skills that separate the experienced climber from the weekend recreationalist. I could handle the high-angled rock and its thin holds with confidence. I was comfortable with the equipment and by now could enjoy the airiness of a hard rock climb, and I reveled in the sociability and mutual trust generated by a day on the mountain with friends of comparable experience and commitment. I'd learned the value of patience in examining the next move or series of moves. I could define my strengths as a climber as well as my vulnerabilities. I was competent enough on rock without being the virtuoso that some of the professional guides and great climbers were. But I mastered most of the gymnastics demanded on a major mountain where most of the climbing was on rock—the laybacks, friction, chimneying and the others. Like most climbers I'd acquired a rhythm, where the pitch of the rock permitted, and once I'd graduated into that kind of movement, a good day on a mountain became an absolute carol. Yet I was probably stronger on high angled snow because I could literally climb all day. I loved going upward, punching my crampons into the hard pack, driving my axe into the snow and lifting my face to the wind.

The old fears of inadequacy from my first years in the Tetons had been replaced by the kind of kinship the climber eventually feels for the mountain itself. I don't mean something mystical, off the charts of reality. But you can't look at a great mountain, much less try to climb it, without searching the crannies of whatever poetry lurks in you when you roam to the edge of the stratosphere. Of all of nature's creations, mountains are the mightiest and for most of us they are charged with symbolism. They are the closest to the heavens, to God himself.

Against such attributions, of course, the mountain is essentially defenseless. The mountain simply is. Its appearance or its accessibility changes with the weather, the season, and the time of day. Yet for the climber, the mountain is more than simply dumb dead rock or ice. It is the materialization of a kind of fairy tale. One of the things that makes us most human, the mountaineer and writer James Ullman insisted, is the longing for something that at first seems inaccessible and after all of our search and striving may *be* inaccessible. Yet the search is worth the candle.

On the Matterhorn the Hornli or northeast ridge does not pose any towering technical problems. That is under normal conditions. The Matterhorn's eccentricity has been part of its core character, exciting every mountaineer who has touched it, whether master climber or beginner. It is a mountain of contradictions, a gleaming white pyramid of startling beauty from the valley floor, but a moldering geological slagpile up close. In a storm or for the complacent climber who underestimates its latent strength, it can be a killer at any time, and it has taken the lives of a thousand climbers.

But the Matterhorn closest to me was the Matterhorn of history. That and it's uncanny symmetry and its imagery for those drawn to the high country. And now 15 years after my first experiences on its cliffs and icefields, I met Gottlieb again in 1973 in the dining room of the climber's hut, the ancient pension Belvedere. He looked about the same. The creases under his eyes were a little deeper and his greeting, "*Wie geht's*?" somewhat warmer. We shook hands. I decided this was acceptance that came right to the brink of approval. After 15 years, I marked this down as progress. It was actually a little better than that. We had a dinner of spaghetti and pork chops together at a table looking up at streaks of zinc cloud curling up to toward the Matterhorn twilight. He said to never mind the cloud. The north wind was coming up and it would be a good day tomorrow. He said good night and left for the guide's lodge next door to the climber's quarters for a brandy. Before going to sleep I felt a relative ease. This was still a mountain of mountains, but I knew it better now. I was older and better on a mountain and I found myself in a comfortable zone of readiness.

But the adrenaline was surging nonetheless. At 2:45 there was a clumping on the fissured old floorboards of the Belevedere. Somebody was awake and moving, eager enough to get on the mountain that he risked the reproach of the other climbers who knew the kitchen maid was not due with her wake-up until 3. I couldn't join them in their scowls because I was doing the clumping. I didn't feel apologetic about it until I nearly broadsided the kitchen maid in the darkness. It helped to remember that mountain climbing for all of its fearsomeness and melodrama was still fundamentally an extension of a child's playground game. The difference was that thousand-foot rock walls had replaced the gym poles.

Starlight flooded the great sweep of the Alps and the immensity of the Matterhorn above us when we walked the small snowfield that took us to the first steps on the mountain. The scale of the mountain and that night sky was numbing. And here was the Matterhorn powering its way into the heavens.

"Christos," I had to tell myself.

We moved rapidly through the mountain's lower cliffs and ravines. I was fit and the lower part was a romp. We moved together holding the rope in coils at our sides. If I knew physics I would have called this synergy but I had a second thought. What an awful word to inflict on a mountain climb. The going was so good that I sang a few bars of "It's a Long Way to Tipperrary." I don't know why Tipperrary. Why not? I'd never felt so care-free on a mountain.

We passed a couple of young Japanese climbers, unfamiliar with the route. Gottlieb showed them the way but, when they started to advance, stopped them. "*Eine Moment,*" he said. Wait. They froze. The Bergfuhrer goes first. It was protocol, but it was also Gottlieb. In a few minutes their headlamps were pinpoints hundreds of feet below us. There were others on the mountain. But our climb seemed so crisp and unlabored that we had the sensation, at least I did, of being alone on the mountain. You can't call the Matterhorn's jumbled geography of crags and buttresses graceful despite its appealing profile on a million calendars and chocolate boxes. It has paid the price for its aloofness from its snowy neighbors. Unprotected through the ages, the mountain has been battered by erosive forces of wind, ice and water. So all right, it may be a great slag pile, a geological hag masquerading as a mountain Snow White. And on a sunny day in August it is practically an ant hill of sweating tourist-climbers.

But let's say you go to the Matterhorn often because it has taken on a special significance in your life in wild nature. Maybe it has become a kind of fixed beacon renewing your commitment to the treasure and the thrill of encountering the wild outdoors. And does this create a connection between the seeker and the mountain that is going to be permanent, and never mind if it's romanticized? It does.

So what's wrong with romanticizing a relationship like this one. You and the good earth. Or this one and very special part of the earth. It began the day when I climbed on this mountain uninhibited and discovered the ultimate treasure of the climbing experience once the fear and the awkwardness had vanished. I was climbing free, miles above the sea and 10,000 feet above the village, my body and mind in harmony, the rope loose, Gottlieb skimming the rock and ice a few feet above me, not needing to stake us to the mountain. Miles to the east the day was beginning to come alive. The still-invisible sun was casting its first streams of tentative amber above the Monte Rosa. We used the friction of our boots to climb the smooth Mobley slabs beneath the emergency hut, where we had gnawed on some dried beef for a few minutes before strapping on crampons for the snow and ice cliffs of the fixed ropes above. The lights began to flicker out among the toy houses of Zermatt in the valley and the pale blue of the morning sky spread from Switzerland to Italy to France. It was a magical day, immense and wonderful and intimate. The western breeze was rising, carrying the cold breath of the glacier to the mountain and turning August to winter. The wind strengthened and whipped small slivers of snow and ice into our faces. With it came the first sensation of fatigue. The question was not Why but Where had it been? We'd come nearly 4,000 feet in three hours and now I was standing in my footholds a few hundred feet beneath the summit, sucking in the Matterhorn's cold gale. It had enough force to bite and numb. But that was part of it, wasn't it? There are times when you yearn for tranquility in life and others when you want to feel the force of restless nature and to luxuriate in its sounds and touches.

What is the summit of the Matterhorn without the wind to announce this priceless moment when the snows and slabs fall away and all that was above us was the blue infinity of the alpine sky?

And suddenly above the ridgeline of the Pennine Alps to the east the sun erupted and spread gold and vermilion on the snow slopes, declaring that on this day of days we'd arrived at almost the exact moment when we could witness sunrise from the summit of the Matterhorn.

And what was the climber's reward? To be able to cleanse his sweat with a handful of the Matterhorn's snow, to feel the life and history of this rock of ages, and to see the gruff professional guide standing on the summit with a child's smile at the wonder of that sunrise. And what else? Maybe the cool breath we felt was not only the wind. Maybe there were spirits here after all, dancing in the wind mischievously to join the celebration. Who said ghosts had to be glum?

We lingered on the summit for a few minutes to soak some of the sun's warmth into us, and then Gottlieb coiled the rope and we went down.

We climbed four more times on the mountain, once by the long and difficult Zmutt ridge that was Gottlieb's favorite of all of climbs on the Matterhorn. It got him away from what had become a procession on the Hornli Ridge. It was exacting. You cross the Matterhorn Glacier, then the *bergschrund* where it separated from the rock. You crampon up a steep 800- foot snow pitch, front-pointing the crampons all the way, to a kind of razor ridge where for 300 or 400 yards you climb with your left boot on the Swiss side of the mountain and the right on the side facing Italy. And then up the high angled nose of the Matterhorn's west face to the summit. Later I climbed with others, and once with Rod Wilson, alternating leads.

And now on this Christmas Eve, so many years later for Gottlieb and me, the Matterhorn was behind us as climbers but certainly not out of our lives. We talked for more than an hour, reminiscing. After our talk he was going to spend a few minutes at the steepled old Catholic Church that reaches back to the middle of the 19th century when Zermatt was a hamlet of milk farmers and rough-hewn chalets and cow barns. It still anoints each day in Zermatt with the tolling of its chimes. The sound fills the valley and floats up the mountain slopes and mingles with the Arolla pines. When you're hiking thousands of feet above the village of today, you have to stop to listen to this angelus of the Alps that moves you to give thanks for the innocence of the day, the nourishment and the music of the bells.

And for Gottlieb? Decades later now, he was congenial. "You know, I never got tired of it," he said. "I remember that day on the Zmutt because I felt free. It gave me a chance to climb using technique that you didn't need everyday on the Matterhorn. I almost felt alone on the mountain even though the mountain was there every day of my life in Zermatt. You could climb within yourself. Do you know what I mean?"

I did. And on that final meeting in 2006—when he was 80 and I wasn't far from there—I could confide things that would have seemed gratuitous during our climbs. I told him that I had climbed enough elsewhere through the years but for me the Matterhorn was the Rosetta Stone of the mountains. It defined them. It was the first great mountain I'd ever seen and now it seems to have become a marker in my life, from my first adulthood to what we once called old age. I said, "I remember leaving my name for you at one of the hotels when I asked for a guide in 1958, and we were the only two on the mountain."

And then I told him: "You took thousands of people to the summits. I don't know if you realized that you were opening a new world and commitment for so many of them. It changed their lives." I told him it created for the rest of their lives a bond with a part of the world where their spirits could run with the wind. I said this is what he had done for me, and it was a gift.

He got up to leave. He was not the Teutonic Bergfuhrer I remembered; he was old and warmer and accessible, celebrating now a different time of recognition. We embraced. In the old world manner, he touched my cheek with his, then the other. I gave him a bottle of wine as a holiday gift. I said I already had received his gift years before and it would last a lifetime.

13

The Ultimate Adventure

The Moon, Space, and Heartache

The sky was to starting to cloud on my drive back to Minneapolis after a few days in northern Minnesota late in 1985. I stopped for coffee at a country cafe, where I bought a copy of the morning's *Minneapolis Star-Tribune*, for which I wrote a daily column. Below the fold on the front page was a brief story with photo identifying one of the finalists named the previous day by NASA in its forthcoming journalist-in-space project.

I was the man in the photo.

The man behind the counter had already read the paper. "Congratulations," he said. "You're going into space."

I smiled ambiguously. It seemed like the thing to do. "There are other finalists," I said. "The odds that I'll get there are really pretty long."

"But you'd like to."

I nodded. He was probably going to ask why, a question that was completely logical. But four more customers walked in, ending our conversation.

On the drive home a hard rain came down layered with snow and sleet, allowing me very little time to picture myself strapped into a rocket ship, waiting for the countdown. I had already pretty well exhausted the what-if-it-happens exercises during the weeks of NASA's selection process. Inviting a journalist into space was the next step in NASA's campaign to popularize and broaden public support for its manned explorations. It would come a year or so after the flight scheduled for early 1986, in which Crista McAuliffe, a school teacher, would join the astronauts in the shuttle Challenger.

American space flight had experienced accidents and misfires, but I couldn't honestly name anybody in my business, or any other, who would turn down a chance to fly toward the stars and literally out of this world. And if you happened to be one of those who is aroused by the idea of something beyond in your life, whether a mountain top or a simple turn of the trail, what could be more electrifying than a flight into space?

There had been a day not long before, in 1969, that briefly and profoundly united the world. For a few unforgettable hours it linked all of humanity with the enfolding sight and sudden realization that what was once make-believe was now here, and men walked on the moon.

It was a moment that by almost unanimous agreement represented a lofty journey of the human spirit—perhaps its most majestic.

The astronauts seemed to walk under the glass of eternity, their every movement and word a triumph of the ages. On cue they pronounced the words meant for the world's future antiquarians and parlor game zealots— "that's one small step for man, one giant leap for mankind." But as players in the drama that came after, they seemed closer temperamentally to Tom Sawyer and Huck Finn than to Columbus and Magellan. They frolicked and traded throwaway lines like funsters off on a spree, rather than wary and somber explorers on the watch for lunar quicksand.

A quarter of a million miles from earth, in the black-rock desert of another world, Buzz Aldrin peered at the little hump of rubble in front of him and announced with a bright sense of discovery:

"Neil, I told you we'd find some purple rocks." Neil Armstrong sounded impressed, the way a kid would react if a swamp-prowling buddy had just announced the presence of the biggest bullfrog in the pond.

We were closer spiritually to these first lunar explorers than we expected to be. We were closer as Americans, as citizens of the world, as sojourners-in-the-wings, sharing those miraculous two hours when humanity entered a universe that had once been depicted as an alien place too cold and untouchable, beyond our reach and comprehension.

They were our heroes, but they preferred not to act heroically, which gave the whole enterprise a quality of delight to equal its historic significance. We watched it all on television, enchanted but properly speechless, taken in not only by the immensity of the achievement but by the ease with which twentieth-century technology made us armchair witnesses to it.

It is no rhetorical exercise to say we all walked on the moon with them.

We did so partly because that day was one of the enduring landmarks in history. We were able to share it in an extraordinary way, but also smile because the two who were there made the moon a playground as much as a laboratory. It wasn't so much triumph and solemnity, "we're there first"— although that point could not have been lost on the world.

They were astronauts and scientists and test pilots, all right, but we understood them best when they bounced around on the surface like 12-year-old kids in the first snow. Their pinch-me, we're-on-the-moon discoveries captivated us. "One small step…" will go into the archives but the bigger applause line was the sidewalk slang from Neil Armstrong, "Houston, I'm on the porch."

Time has a way of eroding the cosmic quality of that July day in 1969. The deep-space telescopes and the rovers on Mars have the same effect.

Yet the first moon walk was an adventure like none other. Was it the ultimate? Probably not. Humanity still has a way to go, you would hope. But it was far more than merely a triumph for human technology. Ever since humans became recognizably human, they have looked to the moon both whimsically and metaphorically. We have long considered it to be a mythical body capable of exerting odd influences on young romantics, wolves, and cheese-lovers; and we have often imagined going there. And now, after a few thousand years, we could, and did. We flew a rocket up there, attached a lunar lander, put on a tasteful show for the world and then came safely home. It was better than Jules Verne.

In fact, the event was so extraordinary that it was difficult to grasp during the two short hours of the visit how giddy it all really was.

Armstrong descends warily, dipping a tentative toe into the sand. The heroics out of the way, he jumps onto the moon and practically shouts to Aldrin: "Not a creature in sight."

Like the first tourist photographer ever born, he forgets the time of day and starts shooting pictures despite the gentle prodding from his overseers on earth about scoops of rocks and soil.

Somewhat apologetically, he scurries away from the lunar module (they called it LEM, remember?) and tells Houston, "I think I'll try to get a rock over here." He has been on the moon only ten minutes, but already he is vaguely proprietary, the moon's first public relations man. "It's different," he reveals, "but it sure is pretty here."

And so they frolicked around the module, experimenting with high knee action in the fashion of a pro footballer running to daylight.

It was the ultimate sandlot for the spacesuit athletes from Outer Expressway, and for the golfing duffer it was the biggest bunker in the solar system. At one-sixth gravity, Aldrin must have been dying to try history's first 800-yard wedge shot.

They hustle about loading up a few more rocks which science predicted might unwrap the secrets of the universe. Science fell a little short of that mission but it was time for Houston to tell Aldrin:

"Get on up the ladder, Buzz," Houston says drolly.

He did, and Armstrong followed a few minutes later.

Behind they left a plaque inscribed: "We came in peace for mankind."

I think they did. There are no shooting wars in space. It may be something to remember.

Was it adventure as well as science and mission, somebody asked the astronauts later? Did they feel it, and were they satisfied from the beginning that no matter how it came out, it was going to be worth the risk?

They weren't going to deny any of that. Why would they?

It was something that came up years later, to me personally when I became a finalist in the journalist-in-space venture. Imagine orbiting in space, reporting on the events to an audience of—how many? Two billion?

In applying, I had never honestly considered the risk. The prospect of going into space was too enticing for that. You would be going not only as a passenger but as performing member of the crew, broadcasting the experience, describing the sensation of space, weightlessness, the pure spectacle of space and the receding but glorious globe we called home, sharing the otherwordliness of it.

NASA received 1,700 applications. We wrote papers describing our conception of the role and what we considered our qualifications. I was a newspaper columnist with multi-media experience as the host of a television show for several years and of a radio talk show. I spoke in public in a variety of venues, flew a light plane for 10 years, had parachuted recreationally several times, flown in a balloon and climbed in the Himalayas, Andes, Alps and the American West. If one of the qualifications was experience undergoing stress in novel situations, I suppose my resume compared reasonably well.

NASA conducted a series of eliminations culminating in an interview by a panel of educators, in my case at Iowa State in the north central district.

The final eliminations were to be conducted in Houston. Thirty-four applicants remained. I was one. I looked at a partial list of the others. As I remember it included Walter Cronkite. Assuming his health was normal, I told a friend, he would have been my own first choice hands-down. No one in American journalism deserved the honor more, and the American television public would have loved it. They would have seen Walter in space, Walter who practically immortalized himself in the American space program with his "go, baby, go" during one of the critical launches; Walter with his crackling and authoritative narrations of the crucial early and late stages of the space flights from Florida and then Houston.

Sometime during the selection rounds, an astronaut walked into my office. It was George (Pinky) Nelson, a Minnesotan. He had ridden the shuttle on two space missions and would make a third flight later. He was also the first astronaut to walk untethered in space. On a speaking tour, he stopped at the newspaper and asked about my possibilities in the forthcoming NASA project. He was stimulating and encouraging, recounting his experiences.

He is now an academic doctor on the faculty of Western Washington University in Bellingham, Washington. But on that day he had returned from one of his recent missions with the exuberance of a man seeing the world for the first time. And so he had, the planet Earth in all of its distant marvels, from thousands of miles in the sky.

He said the earth's precise physical features did not quickly reveal themselves. But later he and his crewmates could make out, stretching from the buff sands of the Middle East to the jungles of the south of Africa, the great gash 4,000 miles in length that we call the African Rift.

From closer to the earth they could distinguish lines of brush fires, miles in length, fires the villagers had started in Africa to speed up nature's fertility. It startled them, this distant sight of their world from lifeless space.

A few months later, on a January morning in 1986, I walked into the newspaper's photo lab, minutes after the Challenger flew into space with Crista McAuliffe and a full complement of astronauts on board. A thin column of smoke was snaking its way through the sky from the top of the television screen. Something had happened to the Challenger not long after the launch. We stood and watched, unable to speak.

I wrote the next day:

"The underside of adventure is risk. Telemetry and mission controls cannot alter that unchangeable truth, although for years we convinced ourselves they could. Because the space flights have been so successful, because the upbeat theater they created on television put us in a continuing never-never land of happy endings and smiling, modest heroes, the thought of risk and catastrophe rarely intruded on the show.

"It may explain why the country's grief is so profound today, approaching mass depression.

"It was one more romp in space, this time with an effervescent novice on board, a schoolteacher whose presence in her flight suit seemed to be telling all who watched: "It's OK to dream."

"So far had the space flight technology progressed. The launch, the rocketry, the space plane were safe enough to put ordinary people into the heavens and the unknown. They could travel in space with professionals who had the right stuff, joining them in an orbiting social.

"And then the fireball.

"It was crushing, lethal, and final. It broke an illusion.

"Space flight has been a kind of national toyland for years, where the adventure we were witnessing was played out free of harm to ourselves or hostility to others. A trip to the moon menaced no one. It was competitive, yes. The Soviets were out there. But there was something about the innocence of space that stirred both sides to thoughts of cooperation, and led them there.

"Was there any more powerful symbol of what the divided people of the earth were capable of becoming than the sight of American and Soviet astronauts living and working in the same spaceship, bound to each other by their shared technology and sense of wonder?

"The price tags of space exploration were controversial, and so was the country's proposed militarization of it. But that was heavy budget stuff.
"Space flights were festival, or something very close to it. They entered into the American consciousness as something that brought us some bearable suspense, and then a new wellspring for a national pride and identity. We flew in the capsules with John Glenn and walked on the moon with Neil Armstrong. As one space vehicle after another flew the course on the television screen, year after year, the space flights became a kind of recurring parade in their effect on the public. They were fun to watch, they had a predictable ending, and nobody got hurt.

"Tuesday, in the skies above Florida, the festival shattered and fell into the ocean in a thousand pieces, while millions wept for the buoyant spirits on board who fell with it.

"It was shocking because we had come to rely on the competence of American spacemanship, a reliance that bred an aura of perfection. It had to be right and perfect, or the computers wouldn't let the rocket go. It was on the money and looking great; and then the fireball.

"The finest tribute to what the country's space people have accomplished in 25 years is that it created this very sense of trust and reliance. That will be examined. But people will go aloft again from Cape Canaveral.

"You can argue that we will fly in space because it is part of our defensive preparedness. But that is not the real reason, is it? Human beings will explore in space because since the sunrise of time they have been searching to find what is beyond them.

"Sometimes it brings them marvels. And sometimes they fail.

"These we mourn with special grief today because their dreams were ours."

In the aftermath of the Challenger accident came the Congressional hearings, a description of the probable causes of the accident and a re-commitment to safety and accountability in the American space program.

NASA for a time stepped back from the manned flight program. Then it re-entered. Somewhere during those transitions NASA said the journalist-in-space program had been placed on hold. And, later, the program yielded to the inevitable and was cancelled.

As far as I know, none of those who were still considered potential civilians-in-space were formally notified. The decision and its wisdom were obvious and the idea simply dissolved.

And then on a Saturday morning I stopped at a dry-cleaning shop near my home to pick up an order, and there was excitement and high tension in an announcer's voice coming out of the small television set on a desk.

I'd forgotten that this was the day of another shuttle's return to earth. I was the only customer, and I asked the young attendant if he could turn the screen so that we could both see.

The Columbia was descending, preparing to land in a few minutes. Something was wrong. Mission Control had lost contact with the captain. The *Christian Science Monitor*, to which I contributed after my retirement from the *Star-Tribune*, later asked if I would give my impressions.

I wrote: "Even after the ominous first announcements, it seemed so innocent and clean flashing through the morning sky on our television screens, a streamer of white heralding one more arrival from space.

"Maybe we've seen so many fictional encounters in space that we can't quickly absorb or accept the terrible reality of death in the heavens when it is soundless and comes to us masked as a swift and graceful plume of smoke splitting the blue sky above Texas.

"Space is still a fantasy world for most of us. Its heroes are not warriors or gladiators confronting an enemy in arenas of violence. Space is full of wonder and mystery. It unites our imagination with our longing to reach for and to find something beyond us.

"The instant and global attention that today's television brings to a flight to the moon or to an orbiting safe house in space creates audiences into the billions of people. Yet it remains a personal odyssey for many who watch. The canvas of that journey is huge, the universe itself. Because it is, the event sweeps us for a few moments or a few hours into an experience that dissolves the boundaries of everyday life. It lets us soar and revel in a kind of psychic weightlessness in which we can frolic with the astronauts. It is exhilarating and it seems harmless.

"It is not harmless for the men and women who have become our escorts. But the technology of rocketry and space flight has advanced so far and its success rate is so remarkable that the illusions of the space journey have become part of the spectacle.

"It will all end happily on a runway in Florida, we tell ourselves.

"On Saturday morning, nearly 40 miles above the earth, the illusion broke once more, 17 years removed—almost to the day—from the awful fireball in the sky that ended the flight of the space shuttle Challenger.

"The scientists, the engineers and the astronauts are constantly aware, of course, of the hazards. And the viewing public is reminded of it at each step of the countdowns despite the terse professionalism of those disembodied voices reciting the familiar litanies and dialogue between Mission Control and the shuttle commander.

'Why, then, is the pain and devastation we feel so complete and stunning, so uniquely personal, when the space ship falls in pieces before our eyes? We see grief and tragedy on our screens almost every day. We respond to it with anger or compassion or futility. On Sept. 11, 2001, the death and destruction of an attack on America stirred Americans from sorrow to retaliation and now toward war.

"Death in space is not like that. Although space exploration began as a harsh and expensive duel between the Cold War powers of 50 years ago, there is no special villainy in the stars today. It is a place for the exploring spirit to romp and, incidentally, to do some required research because it gets to be expensive floating around up there. It's the home of quirky contraptions like the space station and lunar modules, and we feel like kids again, watching the action. Schemes for the militarization of space are still on the table, but most of us still look on space flight as almost pure adventure.

"The star wars are make-believe. The actual heroes of space are people who might comfortably be our neighbors, although they know all about the risk and some of them are spurred by that risk. They are competent, brave and not gripped by illusions. Slowly the face of the space crews has changed, so that when we looked once more Saturday morning at the stills of the team that rode space ship Columbia, we were looking approvingly at a kind of family of man. Among the seven were men and women, people of color and a military veteran from Israel.

"They seemed altogether normal and unaffected, no matter how professional. And perhaps that explains why, when the ghastliness of what we were watching came clear, our loss was so personal, why our mourning for their families went so deep.

"What binds them most intimately to us?

"It is what seems to be that uninhibited sense of awe and delight that ignites both the trained astronaut and the obscure trail hiker when the path breaks clear of all of the impediments and the sky is wide open and full of invitation and the view seems to stretch forever.

"The distant skies are not the natural habitat of human beings. But finding out what is around the bend in the road, or beyond the hill, defines part of our humanity, and sometimes it is our dreams that unite the stroller with the explorer.

"And so they did Saturday morning."

We can wake up from dreams. Sometimes the reality that follows our dream is not so kind.

15

Sigurd Olson

A Poet-Guardian of the Silences of the Woods

At last I am beginning to believe I am part of all this life and to know how I evolved from the primal dust to a creature capable of seeing beauty. This is compensation enough. No one can ever take this dream away; it will be with me until I have seen my last sunset, and listened for a final time to the wind whispering through the pines.

—Sigurd Olson, who on his last day
heard the wind whispering in the pines.

He was a tall and slender man with silver hair and a melodic, unhurried baritone voice that seemed in harmony with the commitment that guided his life: the preservation of American's natural treasure that he called "part of the nation's soul."

It was a voice to which millions responded over the nearly 50 years in which Sigurd Olson was the poet-warrior of the conservation movement in America. He was simultaneously an evangelist and a witness, a story teller, a man of science, a man of the woods and a very stubborn, but rather courtly Scandinavian.

The romance of the wilderness, which has attracted increased fervor among succeeding generations of American young people, was the song of Sigurd Olson's life.

He lived most of his life in Ely on the fringes of northern Minnesota's Boundary Waters Canoe Area, which for years was the focus and battle-

(Left) Sigurd Olson. Photo provided courtesy of the Sigurd Olson Environmental Institute at Northland College.

ground of the struggles between conservationists and the multiple-use forces in the town where he lived.

The echoes of that battle have receded, though they haven't entirely disappeared. But in the aftermath of that battle the Boundary Waters remains intact—not a fenced-off museum of wild nature but a breathtaking choreography of lakes and streams and pine forests and wooded islands, with loons flying at twilight sounding their uncanny yodels. People come by the tens-of-thousands to be delivered from the tumult and clamor of life in the twenty-first century.

There are limits on its use, so there is little congestion. The silences of the woods and lakes that Sig Olson revered have been protected by law into the indefinite future. Something very close to the wilderness experience—and it is real— is now available to those who come to these waters, largely because of Sigurd Olson and his allies.

On a January day in 1982, Sig dressed for an hour in the crisp winter of northern Minnesota and was ready to step out into the snow when a talkative friend called. He pretended to chide the caller for delaying the big deal of the day. "I want to get out on these new snowshoes the kids got for me," he said. "Thanks for calling and I'll talk to you later."

He was 82, but still athletic, romping around in the snow, making a trail for his wife of 60 years, Elizabeth. They might have been kids again, impulsively stomping tracks through the evergreen forest behind their home in Ely. They had done it hundreds of times. There was a light cold breeze stinging their faces, but they frolicked in the intimacy of the day and of their lives together.

Not far from his house, Sig Olson, collapsed of a heart attack and died shortly afterward in a hospital.

I learned about his death as I was about to leave Minneapolis to see him. We were going to meet to tape a television piece for a program which later became one of his memorials.

For all of his adult life, Sigurd Olson gave testament to what he called the yearnings of human beings for a sensible reconciliation with the nature that gave them life.

"Deep down in his subconscious," he wrote, "a part of (man's) pool of racial memories is an abiding sense of oneness with life he cannot deny. Within him is a hunger and a craving for wildness and nature, which he

cannot quite understand. He must feel the ground under his feet, use muscles as they were meant to be used, know the warmth and light of wood fires in primitive shelters away from storms. He must feel old rhythms, the cyclic change of seasons, see the miracles of growth, and sense the issues of life and death. He is, in spite of himself, still a creature of forests and open meadows, of rivers, lakes and seashores. He needs to look at sunsets and sunrises and the coming of a full moon. Although he is conquering space and producing life, ancient needs and longings are still part of him, and in his urbanized civilization he still listens to the song of the wilderness."

Sig Olson called this the gift of the Hidden Forest, and that phrase became the title of one of his books. The son of a Chicago minister, Sig experienced that gift for the first time in the woods as a young man while canoeing in Wisconsin. He became a biologist, a guide and later the dean of the community college in Ely, where for a year I was one of his students. In later years he lobbied for the preservation of the wild country, and became the author-statesman of the conservation movement. But Sig was no woolly visionary. He looked at the wildwood not only with a poet's lyricism, but also with a naturalist's curiosity and precision for detail, and these combined values gave him absolute credibility, and made him a worthy successor to Henry David Thoreau and John Muir in bringing to masses of people the power and marvel of the natural world.

These qualities and perspectives also brought him impressive regiments of enemies and opponents, who maintained that commercial interests could be served without debasing the essential virtues of the wild country. The battle was over how much commerce was enough and how much intrusion could be allowed before wild nature basically was shredded of all value as wild nature.

Road builders would have opened the Boundary Waters for honky-tonks in the 1930s and 1940s, the conservationists said. There are no honky-tonks there today. The resort operators in northern Minnesota fought bitterly against protectionists they regarded as patricians trying to create a private Shangri-La.

The combat wasn't especially refined. Olson was hung in effigy in his own home town three years after the community gave him a testimonial dinner.

Passions never linger very far beneath the surface in northern Minnesota.

But Olson temperamentally could not attack his opponents as villainous people. His response was measured and almost invariably courteous. But neither he nor his compatriots gave in to local pressure and in 1975 Congress passed legislation that had the effect of banning motors on 75 per cent of the total lake surface in the Boundary Waters, and today peace more or less reigns.

Throughout the furor, Olson resisted personality battles or attitudes of martyrdom. He recognized that his opponents had a cause of their own, a lifestyle they believed was under attack. But while he was civil, he wasn't naïve. He had a politician's savvy when he found himself in the arena of polemics and he knew that name-calling and recrimination didn't win many wars. Moreover, it wasn't his style. Although he never temporized about the wilderness, he wasn't a brawler. His language was thoughtful and restrained and he made a striking appearance with his tanned good looks and silver hair.

He was as comfortable in the classroom as he was in the hearing room in Washington, but the places that defined his life and his cause were his cabin in the woods near a place he called Listening Point, and the little shack where he produced an extraordinary amount of literature and journalism that told of walks among the birches, vigils beside a backwater stream and reveries on the trail. He was absorbed by the chemistry of man-and-nature, the idea that we still carry in our blood and our genes the awe and dependencies of our ancestors who lived when there was only wilderness. His philosophy flowed both from his science and his poetry, but it was the science, his knowledge of biology and geology, that made Olson so convincing in debate or advocacy.

No doubt it was that other part of him—the poetic part—that appealed to his closest friends and his readers. A friend and ally in his fight to preserve the wilderness, Charles Dayton, saw him as a man who viewed nature as an oracle. "He felt that nature spoke to man of the wonders of the universe," Dayton said. "That is why he describes his peak experiences in the metaphors of sound, and urges us to listen also to "the singing wilderness." In one of his books Sigurd describes the song of the wilderness:

"I have listened to it on misty migration nights when the dark has been alive with the high calling of birds, in rapids when the air was full of their rushing thunder, at dawn with the mists moving out of the bays, and on cold winter nights when the stars seemed close enough to touch. The music can be heard in the soft guttering of an open fire or in the beat of rain on a tent, and sometimes long afterward, like an echo out of the past; you know it is there in some quiet place; or while doing a simple task out of doors."

And again:

"After years of searching I found a place of my own and called it Listening Point, because only when one comes to listen, only when one is aware and still, can things be seen and heard. It would speak to me of silence and solitude, of belonging and wonder and beauty. Though only a glaciated spit of rock on an island-dotted lake with twisted pines and caribou moss, I knew it would grow into my life and the lives of all who shared it with me. However small a part of the vastness reaching far to the Arctic, from it I could survey the whole, hearing the singing of the wilderness, and catch perhaps the music of the spheres."

The progression of life, the history of humanity, and the geological history of the planet itself, Olson believed, could be read by studying the vein of rose quartz at its tip. An old pine stump could reveal the ecology of the plant kingdom. An old Indian legend about the circular movement of time could expose the dreams of all humankind.

If there was any part of him that was a dreamer, it was the part that believed the miracle of humanity's discoveries of its history should be available to all. And they could only be available if there was still something we call the wilderness, a place of repose and personal restoration, whether in the Boundary Waters of northern Minnesota or on the mountain slopes of the Wind River Range in Wyoming.

I knew Sig Olson only in his later years, first as a student, and later as journalist and fellow-townsman, exploring the possibilities in life available (for Sigurd) in the wilderness and (for me) in the adventure of discovery.

I don't know many people on earth for whom I have as much admiration, and now affection. Each page of Sig Olson that I read in my later years, whether it was to revisit some pine-scented reverie from Listening Point or to discover a previously unpublished work introduced in that book, gives me a twitch of regret. The words and harmonies are there. Sig's disposition is there. He is there in every page as minstrel and evangelist and friend, so that reading or rereading Sig Olson remains a renewable feast, full of joy and necessity for those whose values are nourished by his counsel and his companionship.

My regret is not being able to hear the voice of Sigurd Olson. That may not be a reasonable lament. Books can't appease all the senses, even when they are generously touched with poetry, as Sig's are. But among his several rarities, Sig was a writer whose voice fused with his language in a symbiosis that gave an unforgettable vitality and yearning to his message. It was a voice that seemed to evoke the heart and depth of the wilderness and to distill its sounds. It was strong, and wistful. He loved to talk about "the great silences" of the north woods. And when he did, his voice lingered over the words and reached beyond the streams and forests to the horizons, as though his invocations could engulf that world and fill the mind with their imagery.

And, of course, he managed that. He did it with the lyricism of his words and the urgency and conviction of his appeal for the preservation of that wilderness. He did it with the authority of his science and with his stubbornness as a believer. He did it because he understood the power and the rhapsody of the wilderness and the needs of people who went to the wilderness for replenishment or simply for fun. Better than most, he recognized the interdependence of a wholesome humanity and a wholesome nature.

Sig has been gone for only a few years, and because history needs some time for reflection and summary, it may be a while before his name is celebrated among those who gave dramatic change in direction to the society of the twentieth century and beyond. He deserves that kind of recognition. Although for millions of people who feel a warmth and comfort when merely scheming another day in the outdoors, it won't truly be necessary.

Many of them have not heard of Sigurd Olson and may not have read a word he has written, yet an indefinable part of their lives, how they look at themselves and at the world, has been influenced by Sigurd Olson.

I was invited several years ago to a grade school class where the project was to create a list of the ten great men and women of the twentieth century. The object was to identify people whose leadership in the building of a better world, whether in politics, social justice, military, or in the sphere of ideas, had positively affected their times and the times that followed. We began with the conventional short list: Gandhi, Churchill, Martin Luther King Jr., Henry Ford, Roosevelt, people of that level of visibility and impact. We argued over some of those nominees, and we argued more ardently over those on the margin.

I then proposed the name of Sigurd Olson and drew a fog of mystification. They wanted to know who was Sigurd Olson and what qualified him to rank with Gandhi and Churchill.

I replied that this was a personal judgment, but as they grew older and learned more about the earth, its treasures and vulnerability, they would understand why Sigurd Olson was important to them and to millions like them.

They seemed impatient. Here they were caught in a riddle. Why should they be interested in a man named Sigurd Olson? Kids don't like to turn riddles into marathons. Their fidgety fingers said what their squeaky voices didn't: Tell us why Sigurd Olson is a big deal.

In self defense, I organized a seminar and advanced show-and-tell. I invited some of them to tell of their experiences in the woods. They talked about canoeing with their parents, camping by a lake, and listening to the wind. I asked if they thought those were special times. They nodded. Were they so special that you would like to enjoy that experience all of your life and pass it on to your children? So special that you found yourself growing a little at the end of each day, knowing more about the woods and feeling good about listening to the stream, and feeling better about the people traveling with you?

Affirmative nods. I asked another question. Would your world be better or worse if as you grew older you found out that those places were gone, and would never return to your life?

Answers tumbled out rather chaotically, and I returned to Sigurd Olson. This man, I said, was one of those who tried to remind people in the United States and in the rest of the world that those times we spend close to the earth are precious to all of us and that the earth itself is precious to us. It is precious not only because it gives and sustains life and is in danger, but because the wild places of the earth are necessary to us for another reason. There are times in our lives when we must go back to something that is beautiful, simple, and restful. The wilderness is full of wonderful living things, and even if it is new to us, it seems strangely familiar because it is how and where we began.

I explained that Sigurd Olson didn't necessarily originate those thoughts. But because he wrote movingly of them and because he expressed the feelings that growing numbers of people needed to see expressed, he became one of the leaders of the movement to preserve a good earth, both as a writer and a warrior. And it was an idea that eventually reached every person in the country until now it has forced its way into the political debate everywhere in America and around the world. And Sigurd Olson was the embodiment of that idea.

Sometime during those final deliberations in the classroom, Sig Olson made the last cut, and his name joined the Churchills and the Gandhis.

Historians may be harder to convince. But for those whose lives are most intimately affected by Sig Olson's stewardship of his singing wilderness, how important is recognition on that scale? The idea is what matters about Sig Olson, what he preached and how: with his language and ardor, his laughter and adolescent reverence for the time of the voyageurs, his unshakable conviction that something in us dies if we allow the wilderness to die.

I'm absorbed by the sound of Sig Olson's voice because it was my last direct contact with him and my most intimate memory of him. We were going to spend that day in Ely for the television documentary I planned to write and narrate. An illness had created a stammer in his speech, but the vitality of his mind and spirit were still there, and so were his intuitive grace and courtesy.

We set a date. A journalist interviews thousands of people over a lifetime. This was something apart and something personal. We talked several times during those years, but this was to be less a professional visit than a reunion. I don't know any that I anticipated more joyously.

He died on that day in the woods, as thrilled to be there as he had been seventy years before.

I think I remember best his life-long appeal to us to keep returning for the peace we feel in the presence of the earth's gifts. Sig called it our sense of wonder. He referred to it a hundred times. It begins in childhood. And if it is just as strong and compelling in later years, as it was for Sig Olson, then we are truly blessed, because it shelters us from cynicism and meanness. Those were qualities that Sig Olson never quite understood. They never entered his mind.

16

Tiny Letters to the Corinthians
And to a Climber Needing Oxygen at 19,000 feet

Somewhere in Rod Wilson's memorabilia is a very small book, not more than two inches wide, that might have carried him through the most horrific night of a lifetime.

He lay exhausted in a sleeping bag, slipping in and out of consciousness, while a wild Andean wind tore at the tent where a friend and a mountain guide were trying to keep him alive.

Earlier that day we had reached the summit of Nevado Huascaran, at 22,200 feet the highest mountain in the Peruvian Andes. Today he remembers only wisps of the ascent, and nothing of his sensations when we reached the top, or of the moment when he came off a steep ice wall on the descent, slid over a lip of the snow field below it and landed on a shelf of ice. There the rope between us came taut and stopped him.

It wasn't that accident that nearly ended his life. Sometime during the climb Rod was overtaken by pulmonary edema, a sickness caused by a lack of oxygen that climbers sometimes experience in the upper altitudes . It is often fatal. When it reaches critical stage it can only be reversed by quick descent to thicker air or by a massive infusion of oxygen, which isn't often available.

The guide, Fausto Milla, and I walked arm and arm with Rod on the descent to our overnight campsite at 19,000 feet. The camp, in the broad saddle called Garganta between the two summits of Huascaran, was being pounded by a gale. Rod was a big guy, not easy to maneuver in the wind on

(Left) A climber (Jim) attacks a steep snow slope in the 22,220-foot Huascaran in the Andes of Peru. The summit is still four hours away. The climbers got there, nearly exhausted by the equatorial sun.

slick snow. He was conscious but groggy and stumbling. The wind was rising, rattling the tent walls and bending the fiberglass poles as we approached. The night was here, and Rod had no strength left.

We got him into his sleeping bag and tried to make him comfortable while we decided what was the best chance of saving his life. It was nearing 9 o'clock at night. Some 5,000 feet below us at our base camp was an oxygen bottle we had stashed in a cave along with our extra gear. We had taken it on the climb strictly as an emergency. Huascaran, although high, normally can be climbed without oxygen as long as the climbers are prudent about managing enough time to acclimatize on the ascent. We had allowed for that. But sometimes that is informed guesswork, deciding how much is enough. There are no electrocardiograms on a mountain

I removed Rod's down jacket and his boots and propped a pillow under his head. The wind outside the tent was constant and savage. In spite of it, you could hear Rod Wilson gagging and snuffling.

Rod and Fausto slept for an hour or so. I got up every few minutes to check on Rod's condition. It was impossible to know whether he was resting, sleeping or drifting off. I called his name several times. When he didn't respond, I woke him up. He sat up and spoke in a voice that seemed drained of all animation. Yet there was a kind of toneless, bizarre thread of dignity and apology in it.

He said he thought he was dying.

He said there was water in his lungs; he could hear himself gurgling when he tried to breathe. He didn't know where he was and he felt himself drifting. He said he had to tell us.

I put a flashlight on his face and pulled the stethoscope out of our first aid pouch. To get acquainted with our bodies' norms we had listened to each other's heartbeats and breathing rhythms a half dozen times. The first time was in the Monterrey Hotel room in Huaraz at 9,500 feet and then at each of the overnight camps on Huascaran.

Pulmonary edema is characterized in part by gurgling in the lungs when the victim breathes. Rod's face was gray, puffed, and expressionless. It revealed neither fright nor pain. I put the stethoscope under his lungs and on his back. I don't know how the medical people define gurgling in the lungs. I heard a crackling when he breathed. I had no training to judge its severity. I did know he was disoriented. His own diagnosis of his condition seemed accurate. Listless and hallucinatory, he looked like a man about to die. We couldn't just sit there and let it happen. There was another tent about 400 yards away on Garganta. I shook its roof. The occupants were a Swiss climber and his girl friend. He gave me a capsule containing something that sounded like a diuretic from the climber's description. I returned to our tent, broke the top of the capsule with a pair of pliers and extracted the medicine with a syringe.

Rod rolled over face down, and I emptied the needle in his bottom. He didn't cringe or groan. He said, "Thanks, doc," and lost consciousness.

Fausto Milla was up and exploring the Garganta terrain for additional help. On the far side of the saddle he found another climbing team, a guide and client. He asked the guide if he would join him in the descent to our base camp 5,000 feet below. That was nearly a mile down on snow and ice seamed with crevasses. By daylight the crevasses can be easily identified and flanked or crossed on snowbridges. At night, for a climber moving quickly on an emergency mission, the only light would be a headlamp strapped to his forehead.

Fausto Milla shook my hand, grabbed a couple of oranges, crawled out of the tent and strapped on his crampons. With his companion, he began the 5,000-foot descent through the night wind and glacial crevasses for an oxygen bottle that seemed a millennium away.

Not long after they'd left, I explained the plan to Rod and said that it would be several hours before they got back but that the oxygen was almost certain to have an immediate effect in restoring his breathing to close to normal. He nodded lethargically, trying to be appreciative.

He then asked me to dig out the little book from his vest pocket. I did and discovered the smallest New Testament I'd ever seen, its print barely readable without a magnifier.

Rod asked if I would read a few passages. I asked for his preferences. He said I could choose what I wanted. I thought this might be a good time to break out a grin meant to suggest the obvious: that I was not a biblical scholar. Rod probably understood that. "Anything would be fine," he said. I thought I would probably detour around Revelation, with all those horns and thundering.

I told Rod I liked what Paul wrote. He nodded.

I read by the light of our overhead lantern: "Love is patient; love is kind; love is not envious or boastful or arrogant or rude. It does not insist on its own way; it is not irritable or resentful. It bears all things, believes all things, hopes all things, endures all things."

I told Rod I thought Paul was writing about hope as a part of love in our search for personal peace, and our need to endure to nourish hope.

Rod nodded. He asked me to read more. I did, intermittently. His eyes closed again. I listened, and he was breathing. But I could still hear the sound in his lungs. This was a man I'd admired from our first ventures into the mountains, and later as a friend with whom I traveled in the Alps and the Himalayas. He was nearly 20 years younger, but mature and sensible, scrupulous as a lawyer and in his personal life. Later he would become a husband and father, a man of faith but also a guy who laughed easily and played a powerful game of golf.

For Fausto, descending now through the labyrinth, leading Rod through those crevasses at night to reach the oxygen would have been impossible, even with an assisting guide. Rod didn't have any strength. They would have had to descend hand in hand with him the whole way. It would have taken an entire day, and he would almost certainly have collapsed before they reached the oxygen.

It was going to take the guides at least nine or ten hours, I was sure. I sat up and did what I could. I'd wake Rod every 15 or 20 minutes. He was warm enough. We talked about the climb to the summit, but he was no help there. He remembered practically none of the details. I'd read again for a few minutes. And I did my own review of the past few days, astonishing as they were.

There were five of us at the beginning, Doug Kelley, Rod Wilson, Fausto Milla (the Peruvian guide), Jacinto(a porter), and me. Kelley was the best mountaineer among us. Doug, Rod and I had climbed together before. The two of them were lawyers and powerful climbers, Kelley a confident tiger in the courtroom, Rod a little more precise, methodical, a marathoner and a marvelous friend

The mountain had looked enormous as we worked our way through the tropical forest and the avocado groves, even more gigantic and unearthly from our base camp at 14,000 feet just below the glaciers. Its snowfields seemed to outreach gravity and rise into the equatorial skies.

In the cave near base camp we stowed our unneeded equipment and a green tank of oxygen that must have weighed 25 pounds. From our camp there we put on our crampons, dug the points of our axes into the ice and moved up on the glacier toward our first snow camp at 17,000 feet.

It was a supernatural place. We walked among great blue grottoes and amphitheaters, icicles 50 feet long, crevasses 300 feet deep. The Andean sun seem to have soldered them into a mural of turquoise, amethyst, and cobalt. The Patagonia pile we wore was steaming quickly, so we removed that and scaled down to one set of underwear and moisture-resistant Gore-Tex pants and jackets

The sun burned through the glacial cream on our faces but we were moving higher and higher, leaping the crevasses and listening to the avalanches rolling down Huascaran North. I could not help remembering George Patton: "God forgive, I love it so."

Andes climbers (from left) Rod Wilson and Doug Kelley paint their faces with zinc oxide to join guide Fausto Milla through high altitude glacial crevasses on Nevado Huascaran.

Have you seen the Andes? Where the Rockies peak out, the Andes's everlasting snow and ice are just beginning. They ride in the sky above the jungle and above the sea in their startling architecture. Here is Alpamayo, hurling its summit to the sun like a white diamond. Near it is a massif of connected peaks laced with ice ridges that give it the look of some celestial suspension bridge. And then Huascaran, the highest in Peru, although hardly the prettiest, actually a double mountain separated by a high saddle at 19,000 feet, La Garganta. Garganta is the threshold to an ascent either on the north side or the true summit to the south, Huascaran Sur, which is where we were headed. It has the classic contours of a mountain, but it is too huge to be loved. Unless one encounters a storm or loses the route, Huascaran does not demand gymnastic technique. In some places it is a slog and a grunt, although in others it offers the airiest kind of pleasure to the mountaineer.

A dense fog clung to our camp at 17,000 for two days, shutting down any upward movement, although it was perfect for acclimatizing. We killed time by tearing a paperback thriller into three sections, each trading his section to the others when we finished. Kelley got the first section, Wilson the second. I got the third. This meant that I knew the solution to the crime on my first reading which, of course, made the other sections irrelevant; So I watched moodily while they read; or I brushed my teeth for the fifth time.

Doug Kelley had developed a stomach sickness on the first day at base camp. He was sick the next morning, worse than the day before, meaning he was queasy and inert. In his natural ambience, Kelley is a sportive, chattering man-about-the-world, filled with the confident lawyer's wit and irreverence and the ex-Green Beret's pride in his musculature and stamina. He is also one of the best climbers in the United States, a sophisticate in the use of all the Yosemite rock-climber's jangling hardware.

None of that opens doors in the Andean stratosphere. The reaction of the body to its thin air is unpredictable, although we tried to take all available precautions. An Adirondack backpacker might go as high as the jets but a muscle beacher might fall into a stupor 7,000 feet below him. Doug was laboring at 16,000 feet, grabbing for air and his insides were already knotted from an unsuccessful bout with breakfast at Camp One's 14,600 feet. He upbraided himself and searched for explanations. By the time we reached 17,000 feet on the glacier, he was dragging.

He struggled against the nausea and torpor sucking him down, and tried first to overpower it and then out-talk it. During the time we were weathered in at Camp Two, Kelley scarcely took solid nourishment. He pretended. He was sly. He would grab a couple of spoonfuls and then walk around the tent unsteadily, dumping the rest of the contents of his canteen when he thought nobody was observing.

His compadres observed.

He would wake up in the morning announcing he had experienced a miraculous rehabilitation. But he almost never left the tent, and his face began swelling under the eyes. His lips were thick and crusted and he looked consummately miserable and sick.

Doug struggled into his climbing clothes when we were ready to go the next morning, and then sat on his pack, distant from the others.

"Take what you need from my gear," he said finally. "I'm going down. I'm too weak to climb, and there's no use holding you up."

He did not sound or look very heroic, but a climber will understand the fundamental sacrifice. Indirectly or silently, he might have invoked some musketeer's code requiring all of us to go down and await his recovery. Big expeditions would never allow that indulgence, but there were only three of us on Huascaran, and we had embraced the idea of this climb for months. We thanked him with concern, and he wobbled off down the glacier with Jacinto.

Above Camp Two vaulted the technical crux of the climb, a 450-foot icefall where the glacier broke over a series of rock cliffs. Wilson and I roped with Fausto and began chopping a route up the wall with our axes and crampons. Halfway up it occurred to me that Wilson's bad leg must make this exercise painfully awkward. He had wrenched his knee six weeks before, jumping out of a canoe, and it was still stiff.

I asked him about it on the icefall, and got the same tape-recorded answer he had been giving us for weeks.

"Good," he said.

"That's some summation for a lawyer," I said.

"It was the best I could do on short notice," he said.

We cleared the icefall, waded hip-deep in soft snow on the ascending slope for an hour, and encountered the Garganta's predictable gales a half hour before reaching Camp Three.

The winds had accelerated to something close to 60 miles an hour by the time we reached the campsite at 19,000 feet, still at least one day and 3,200 feet below the summit. Pitching Kelley's dome tent under these conditions compared in raw aggravation with installing an overcoat on a three-armed man. When you got part of the fabric under control, a loose end would billow and flap and threaten to launch all three of us into the stratosphere.

By 6:00 p.m. we had eaten the chef's specialty (mine), freeze-dried beef Stroganoff from the shelves of Midwest Mountaineering, and were snugly fortified against the wind.

While the nylon crashed and the fiberglass poles twisted and doubled, I lay in my bag, taking an inventory.

The night before a high climb is a time for that. It should avoid melodrama but still acknowledge that this is an alien place for man and could never be completely controlled. I gave thanks for the good that had come to me, and hoped that whatever good I had done partially compensated for the injuries I had caused. I thought of both the love and regret I'd experienced, and when I finished I was content.

The wind subsided by morning. It was going to be a gaudy winter's day in the Andes and it was going to be hot despite the four-mile altitude.

Wilson said he was eager and ready, and established this beyond all dispute by throwing up his breakfast.

We were going for the summit. It floated above us, silver and metallic. And the scene seemed almost to need a symphonic overture. We didn't hear music. But if you can translate orchestral arpeggios into ice cliffs, that is what we were seeing.

Rod Wilson today doesn't remember any of this. After one hour we were heaving for air with almost every stride, fighting the 20,000-foot altitude. In two hours we had to resort to grubby goals: Twenty-five strides, and then breathe for a minute. Maybe two, or three. Wilson, trudging behind me, was tiring. He'd never fully recovered from the leg injury of six weeks ago. But Fausto Milla, in his Cordillera wisdom, had decided on the additives needed to get us to the top: a heavy supper the night before. Eat everything in sight. We tried. What about water? The gringos weren't raised in the Cordillera or the Incans' adobe. They needed at least four quarts of liquid a day to keep going.

Fausto Milla had packed two quarts of water in a plastic canteen, for three people, for a 3,200-foot ascent, and descent, on a hot equatorial day four miles above the sea in the Andes Mountains. Some climbers quench thirst all day with ice. Fausto had that figured. But Wilson doesn't, I discovered.

At 21,000 feet he asked for lip balm. I pulled a tube of Lip Ivo out of my pocket and, absently studying it, discovered for the first time that the raspberry-flavored ointment we had been smearing on our lips was manufactured in Minneapolis. Alms from Hiawatha. The high sun ignited the snowfields and flung the glare and thermal power into our goggled faces. Fausto and I swabbed on another layer of zinc oxide, and Wilson drenched himself in some high-powered sun screen. The track was firm, but endless. How high is the sky? We resumed. Now we were down to 20 strides and recuperation. When Wilson would suck in all the air he could, he called "yo," and we moved again. Fausto Milla, a great guy who hit it off well with his amigos, tried encouragement. He tugged on the rope that connected us. I yanked it back to us and cheerfully told Fausto to piss up the rope. I walked up to him and said, "Fausto, we're gringos. We're going as fast as we can. If we can't breathe, we can't walk." Fausto grinned sympathetically. I apologized. The little man was still an amigo. He yanked the rope again.

At 4:05 p.m. we mounted the little snow dais decorated with orange flags left by an Austrian team and stood on the summit of Nevada Huascaran, 22,200 feet above the sea. We hugged Fausto Milla and said, "Gracias."

We started down. Rod, almost out of it, nearly slipped into one of the deepest crevasses on the mountain. We held him on the rope, he dusted off and kept plodding downward. A hundred strides, then gulp air. Swab on some lotion, anywhere. The face, the wrists, only do it very fastidiously to buy more time.

He never complained. But it was taking forever. By nightfall we were still nearly an hour above the Garganta's plateau and Camp Three just below it. Fausto had lost all of his impatience and was generous and thoughtful at the sound of Rod's wheezes. We got off the slope and were now walking the plateau toward camp, toward a conflagration of stars, toward the Southern Cross.

And then Rod grew worse, and the wind came up, and the long night began.

What I remember most vividly of that night more than 25 years ago was not the dramatic aftermath of the climb and Rod's exhaustion, but his simple request for the little book when he seemed to be losing the struggle.

That, and the vigil for the return of Fausto. Rod was weakening as the early morning wore on. It was obvious. I didn't know how to treat his exhaustion and the apparent extreme altitude sickness. I remembered one of the doctor's creeds: To do no harm.

I looked at my watch a hundred times. It is 1 a.m., 2 a.m., talk to Rod for a while. Wake him. Read. 3 a.m. 4 a.m. I thought about the days with Fausto.

In time, we would love Fausto. He called us amigos. His scrambled, breakneck Spanish and highland patois could not accommodate the names of Doug, Rod, and Jim, and his English was an outright surrender. His copper face was a reconciliation of the races of man, reflecting the broken visions and struggles of the centuries, the elfin innocences and the leathered wariness. Yet for all that he was bouncy and sociable. His ancestries sprang from the islands of the mid-Pacific, the Indian clans that flowed from them, the Spanish gold-diggers who conquered them, and the undefined nations that gave his features a timeless universality.

He was listed in the expedition registries of the Andes as a guide-porter, but this was shamelessly inadequate. He was also part burro and part roadrunner. He had the tinkerer's soul of a garage mechanic down to his last cotter pin . He smiled with the simple radiance of the rising sun and he was the team morale man in the tent, quizzing his clients about their love lives and their gastronomic prejudices. But on his home terrain, the glaciers of the Cordillera Blanca, he was despotic and rude. If you hired Fausto Milla to escort you through the crevasses, suppress anything as offensive as an original thought.

However, he carried a ton.

There was practically nothing in the smorgasbord of camping and mountaineering gear that could not be borne, voluntarily and eagerly, on Fausto Milla's back. He was 32 and could not have weighed more than 135 pounds, but there were days when he carried close to a hundred. If you proposed to relieve him of a few of his burdens , Fausto Milla scowled and dismissed the suggestion as the dumb notion of a tenderfoot. As a climber he was sure and brave, but dangerously primitive in his rope management techniques and his conceptions of axe work. Beyond all he was an amigo, a friend, almost always optimistic but, at the critical times, direct. He wanted to reach the summit, but it was still a day's work if he didn't. It all depended, he said, on tiempo, the weather.

If the weather is bad tomorrow, if it is too cloudy in the La Gaganta saddle or an Andean hurricane is blowing on the route, we stay in the tent. If it's good, we climb. If it's bad for two or three days, we go down. The equation was compact and impossible to misunderstand.

Rod drank some hot chocolate at 7 a.m. but in movement and speech he was fogged and disoriented, acting only on instinct, not wanting to impose. He spoke tonelessly to people who weren't there and talked about the impending try for the summit, vowing he was strong enough to make it. By now he must have lost at least 20 pounds.

I had scooped out a fresh batch of ice and snow to boil on the Optimus shortly before 9 a.m. when somebody twanged, "Hey, gringo."

Fausto Milla materialized with the crate of oxygen.

I grabbed it when he came through the flap and hugged Fausto. Then I unhooked the oxygen bottle from the crate and fixed the nosepiece for Rod. I turned the valve, and pure oxygen flowed into his lungs for 30 minutes.

Imagine Fausto. Down perpendicular ice in the middle of the night, past Camp Two, threading through crevasses unroped the length of the two-mile glacier, he descended 5,000 feet, retrieved the oxygen bottle and retraced the route 5,000 feet up. He had done it all in less than half a day, three or four hours ahead of what I thought was a reasonable timetable. ""Is bueno?" he asked Rod.

"Bueno," Wilson said. He took oxygen at intervals for the next two hours, and then we roped up with two relief porters from Camp One for the descent of the ice fall.

His pulse was close to normal by the time we reached Camp Two, and at Camp One the next day, he was eating again. We conscripted a horse for Rod on the descent to the village of Musho where the proprietor of the little cafe on the dusty main street, by a freak of coincidence, happened to be Fausto Milla.

His cook came with hot soup and rolls, with an entree of rice and creole sauce and sauteed chicken. There were meats in the soup that were sweet but palatable, and I didn't have the nerve to ask their origin but I know they weren't beef, pork, or veal, or anything close.

"El Condor pasa, Fausto," I said with some vague philosophical urge.

"Si," he said gravely.

I went outside, extracted my ice ax from the pack, and handed it to Fausto. Rod did the same with his glacier glasses. The Peruvian's brown eyes expanded and shone. Behind him was a little Indian girl with her bright costume and shawl and funny square hat, for whom I had plucked a flower on our way into Musho.

She had a flower for me.

And it occurred to me that one little native girl's smile can melt much snow and ice, and sometimes the best and most enduring discoveries do not require an ascent to 22,200 feet. They can be in the valley on the face of a little girl.

17

Magellan on a Bicycle Seat

Around Lake Superior in Seven Days, Needing a Samaritan, and Finding One

If you want or need to ride a bicycle 1,100 miles in seven days around Lake Superior, a certain unshackled optimism is allowable. It's probably mandatory.

It's the kind of attitude the psychotherapists would approve: Throw down the barriers and let your mind romp free. You can ride with fantasies if you want, because your vehicle—the over-the-road bicycle—encourages it. You are alone, the bike is a kind of flimsy but willing steed, you are wheeling hour after hour through a shifting landscape, and the sheer spontaneity is irresistible. You are an inquisitive vagabond and you are going to be an oddity on the high-speed highway.

So you can pick the identity of your choice. I found out quickly how amazingly well that worked. Do 6-year-old kids in the Michigan mining town of Wakefield race after your bike, waving their balloons? Adjust your hat and hum a few bars: You're the Pied Piper on Wheels.

And a few hours later, as the ebbing sun spreads the western sky with mauves and blood reds, you can ride the barren asphalt into the clapboard town of Ewen and hitch your machine to the white railing in front of The Hotel. That was the name.

Did Bat Masterson enter Dodge more convincingly?

You're a cowboy, a lone hand, carefully appraising the town. Adjust your hat once more and rub the dust off your nose. Bring your hand down to your waist, but do it unobtrusively. How else do you reach for a tube of lip ice?

To truly enjoy 1,100 miles in seven days around this subarctic Mediterranean, a free-floating imagination is your sanctuary because the reality is dominated by creaky joints, inflamed tendons and spells of misty vision induced by rivers of sweat..

You can't settle for the limited role of a grubby hiker. You are conquistador, beachcomber and fortune hunter. You are voyageur and missionary, roustabout and pilgrim. The label on your 10-speed may read Schwinn (this was in the 1970s) but you know it is more than a bicycle. It is a dependable little Old Paint, living on oil and transfusions of air at the service stations. On command it will change character and become the flying carpet of the Arabian myths, lofting you through the exotica of Lake Superior's geography: Negaunee, Au Train, Michipicoten, and Nipigon.

Is it an ordeal on a bobbing bicycle seat, every day for 150 miles a day?

No, no, it's not that. This is you and the Big Sea Water. Every day a new mood and new weather, new shorelines, marvelous outlooks and gut-busting hills. You do not want to accept the sympathy of automobilers as they streak by you on the shoulderless highway, although you might want to thank them for keeping their bumpers out of your rump.

Let the sympathy run the other way. When was the last time an Oldsmobile driver coasted soundlessly around a bend in the road on Agawa Bay at 5:30 in the morning and found himself confronting an enormous moose, breakfasting in the reeds? When you ride a bike, the moose doesn't disappear. You don't scare him. Plus, he's probably lonely. Good morning, moose.

He had a rack of horns that belonged in the Smithsonian. These he lifted in all of his imperial hauteur and peered clinically at the oncoming bicyclist. I slowed respectfully. I did more than that. I just plain stopped, not only to admire this great beast but to figure out which way he preferred to go. He clearly had the home field advantage. His jaws resolutely worked through a few bales of shoots he had dredged up, he lifted his horns once more and stomped through the swamp without a suggestion of haste. Why should he hurry? Tell me, who is going to crowd a ton-and-a-half moose at 5:30 in the morning?

The cyclist's voyage around Lake Superior is flush with this kind of discovery. He places himself at the whim of the wind and finds himself rewarded with some sudden scent of the forest or sculpture of the shoreline cliff. I asked myself a question about that. Why am I so pleasantly absorbed by all this if I'm breathing so hard?

The answer wasn't complicated. These were private moments. The ride around Lake Superior wasn't a spokes-and-gears version of a marathon. The privacy with the big water and the forests and cliffs around it—that was the point of it all. So let's say this is the reward: hours alone with the Superior sea, the sun rising, watching the moose, taking in the rocky palisades, marking my own time, putting my feet in the water when I biked down to the shore. If you consider that the reward, and I did, you aren't going to find those moments unless you dig liberally into your reserve tanks.

For the cross-country bicyclist the discovery and the vagaries and trials of your anatomy are half of the experience. One part is the odyssey itself, the logistics of it, the gawking at some stupendous rock wall leaping out of the sea and the infinite white border of the highway stretching to the horizon.

The other part is the performance of the body, because the bicyclist who is not bionic will be the first to concede that 150 miles a day on a bike for seven days is an abnormal act.

This I conceded early. And yet I looked at it this way: Here was a reasonably well conditioned guy who happened to be fascinated by the Lake Superior sea, by the poetry of it going all the way back to Longfellow and to my childhood, when Lake Superior for me WAS the sea. It was the sea with its furies in high wind, frozen silence in winter; the enigma of it—an ocean-like body of water too cold to swim in, not very exciting for the fisherman and brutal on the sailor who misread the weather.

In later years when I wrote about it, I said it needed a friend.

And so it had one. In May of 1975, I looked at my calendar and told the newspaper's managing editor: "How about a series on one man's bike ride around Lake Superior?"

Whatever their other considerable virtues, I found this about newspaper editors: as a class they are wary, unfriendly to the idea of having to say yes or no without consulting the financial officer, and practically always in a hurry.

"What's it going to cost?"

"My meals and a round-trip train ride to Superior, Wisconsin."

"Why are you starting in Superior instead of Duluth?'"

"Superior needs a friend, too."

He thought a week to ride a bike around Lake Superior was off the wall, but he conceded that where most people avoided the irrational in making plans, I seemed to pursue it.

The rest of the summer happened to be booked and the last week of May was perfect before the tourist regiments headed up north.

After the first 170 miles from Superior to Ewen, Michigan, I found my body becoming a kind of self-designated laboratory. I could ride 40 miles or so on the straight and level without having to rest more than a few minutes, but on the big hills I experimented with the gears to stay upright and still log reasonable time. Every two or three miles I put one of my hands behind my back to flex the fingers and shake out the numbness. Every hour or so, if the road paralleled the shoreline, I rode down to the water, dunked my bare feet, and sat to watch the ore boats or listen to the robins. My favorite rest-time pursuit was to watch the ingenious aerobatics of the gulls. I wanted to stay on, but there was Wawa ahead.

Have you heard of Wawa?

Wawa is in Ontario, Canada. It's one of those towns that has the sound of a cartographer's practical joke or a bugler's epitaph. It is actually a lively commercial center near the northeastern coastline of Lake Superior. I'd begun the ride on a Saturday morning in Superior, rode 170 miles through the woodland and mining country of northern Wisconsin to Ewen in northern Michigan, camped in a public park and snarfed pizza for supper, then added 155 miles the next day to a second camp-site at Shingleton, Michigan. On the third day I wheeled over the Sault Ste. Marie international bridge into Canada. My next destination was White River, inland to the east of Lake Superior. I rode first to Wawa but from there to White River it was going to be a drag through lovely but essentially hateful country for a bicyclist—gaining 300 feet, losing 400, gaining 500, losing 300. The question was which would come first, saddle sores or sea sickness.

You need to know that the relationship between bike riders and conventional traffic in those years was not as forgiving as it's become today, on either side. In the 1970s bike riders tended to be goal-oriented, blindered and relatively feisty protecting their share of the road. Automobile drivers and truck drivers tended to be scornful—and protective of their share of the road. While I was climbing the endless Montreal River hill an 18-wheel driver began hammering the air horn a quarter of a mile behind me, announcing his strong wishes that I should disappear. The road had no shoulder. I was riding the white line next to bushes two feet high. He kept hammering the horn. When he passed me his passenger window was open. I called him every uncomplimentary name I could think of on short notice. At the top of the hill he had stopped his rig and was standing there with his hands on his hips and his legs spread wide as I huffed up. He told me what he thought about crazy, suicidal bicyclists who slow down traffic. He added some four-letter clinchers. I was more charitable, offering the view that he was a gourdhead and a bastard. Outside of that I thought our conversation was amiable. We came close to blows but the gulls overhead were putting up a terrific racket and they might have attracted the local gendarmes. Twenty miles later I stopped at a café for lunch. The truck driver happened to be sitting on the stool next to me. We stared at each other ominously, after which one of us broke out laughing, the other followed suit, we shook hands and flipped to see who popped for lunch.

Wawa was on the coastline about halfway to Green River. Its skyline is adorned by the statue of a gigantic goose. I was certainly impressed by the goose, but for the long-range biker the most memorable feature of Wawa is its mathematics. Wawa was 66 miles north of the nearest service station and 58 miles south of White River, which was the next identifiable oasis of humanity along Highway 17.

I left Wawa at 4:45 p.m. with the intention of making White River before nightfall, because I had to phone my office and because I had no night-riding equipment. I made the one ten-minute stop for a sandwich, candy bars and water. I lost the coin flip to the trucker and paid for both but ordered mine to go. I shared it with some convivial gnats on a pretty overlook beside a lake. The terrain was woodsy and hilly but highly negotiable for the bicycle and I ground out the miles, stimulated by the run against time and comfortable enough in the evening cool.

When I reached an overlook three miles south of White River it was 9:30 and 20 minutes of straggling light were still available. I rolled onto the shoulder to dismount for a minute to loosen up.

I sank to my knees involuntarily. My legs refused to hold me upright. It was a kinky sensation, trying to rise but being nailed to the ground by some rebellion of gravity. I floundered around on my hands and knees for a couple of minutes while a half-dozen motorists sped by, evidently convinced I was performing some oddball penance or looking for angleworms.

My knees responded after some coaxing. But my legs seemed disconnected, as though they belonged to somebody else.

When I started pedaling again the mysterious paralysis cleared. The knees regained rhythm eagerly, like some hypnotized bongo players grooving on the cadence. The Achilles tendon in my right leg stung from some abuse the day before. To straighten my fingers from the stiffened claws they had become in 13 hours of clenching the handlebar, I had to pry them open manually.

But the demands of convalescence were modest. Five hours in the sleeping bag delivered all of the needed therapy. By sunrise the next day my body was serviceable again and actually revealed symptoms of vitality.

Why not? If you accept the aches and wrenches as a condition of the journey, the road is not your adversary but an actual liberation. Highway travel by car long ago intimidated us with its speed and luxury. We seal the windows, turn on the air conditioning and watch the forest race by. We make the obligatory stops beside a waterfall and five miles later do the same at the flashy Exxon station, because the waterfall's power of suggestion has forced us into the johns. It's a fascinating cycle that tells us much about the phenomenon of natural drainage.

But the bicyclist blends and interacts with the environment, cheering the sun in the early morning, reviling it in the mid-afternoon, riding the wind, attacking it, scenting the spruce stands, establishing a fleeting kinship with the springing deer, tasting the honest dust and being humbled by the might of the Superior sea.

The soul of this lake is gray and aloof, as though it is accustomed to being feared and viewed at a distance.

But I wasn't riding at a distance. I was hugging its shoreline and saying: I'd like to get acquainted. Lake Superior sometimes presents the traveler with a surface loveliness. But it is more honest when it hurls its cold wind against the shore and sends the traveler reaching for another wrap. Yet there is nothing wrong with a nature that is grim in its most characteristic moods. Nobody said it has to be rainbows and moonbeans and sequins on the water all the time.

Traveling alone, you are a self-propelled explorer, a realization that can have a heady flavor. You are captain and crew, the navigator, lookout and, if it comes to that, the chaplain.

Heading into my last day I was going to be smothered if I looked on the ceaseless pedaling as a drudgery. I found it a lot more hospitable to accept it as the trade-off for the sensation of traveling into unearthly mists in the morning at Rossport on the Canadian shore. And then bursting into the sunlight when suddenly the world and life revived and it was a gift to be racing along with the now-carefree surf at my side, joining the frivolity.

My axiom as a wanderer in faraway places has always run something like this: If you are at peace with the places where you travel and willing to absorb the aches to appreciate them, sooner or later something totally unexpected and good is going to creep in to perform a rescue in the crisis.

My crisis came at midnight before the last 160 miles back to Superior. It took the form of Andre, a Native American boy at Grand Portage on the American side of the border. Andre was on duty at the service station where I stopped at 9 p.m. after a long run from Thunder Bay in Ontario. The rear tire was leaking. I asked Andre if he could service the tire. He was a buoyant and willing kid, 17, not hugely experienced. Right, he said, I can do that. While he was fiddling with the valve, he blew the tire.

I looked at the shredded rubber without enthusiasm. Starting at 6 a.m. I would have to ride over Mt. Josephine, a steep rise of hundreds of feet, and after that 150 miles to Duluth, over the bridge and into Superior.

"Do you have anything to replace it?" I asked Andre.

"Not exactly."

"Anything close?

"Not really. I mean, we don't have bike parts."

I'd used my last spare tire late the previous day at Nipigon. Grand Portage was locked up for the night, including the motel. Andre was desolate. I tried to console him and told him I'd try to think of something in the morning. I thanked him for trying and told him to close up and go to bed. He asked me to leave the bike, and I put up my tent in a patch of grass nearby.

At about 2 in the morning I looked out through the tent flap and saw the light still on at the service station.

At 3 in the morning I heard rattling. It was Andre, with my bicycle.

"I think I fixed it," he said.

"Way to go," Andre, "I said. "How much do I owe you?"

"One dollar." He said it was what the station charged to rent the tent ground.

I was amazed. I said it had to be more. I said he worked for four hours, maybe five. It could have been six. "It was my fault," he said. I pointed out that in the cities we pay hundreds of dollars for mistakes, and call this balancing the economy. I strong-armed him into taking more and retired to my tent.

In those years, nothing much stirred at Pigeon River after midnight except for a half dozen revelers at the general store and the tavern. Somebody's lonesome German Shepherd curled up in front of my tent. It wasn't clear which one of us was being guarded.

Mt. Josephine, a mile south of the river, does not thrill the bicyclist with its scenic regality, mostly because you have to pedal up and over the monster. I examined Andre's handiwork one more time. The rubber was firm but the old and rather slight wobble was unreformed. So I attacked the hill, prepared for a war to exhaustion. But the bicycle scarcely broke stride. I got some chirping from the rear tire but there was nothing disabling.

So I just flew up Mt. Josephine in sixth or seventh gear (this was a 10-speed; today you can get 30) and hummed down the North Shore with a song and a yodel. It was less a ride than a celebration, a reunion with Hovland and Tofte and the cascades in the cliffs and the roadside turnoffs in the poplars.

It was the kind of day when the sea revealed its size effortlessly. It needed no musculature today, no pounding and spraying on the rocks. The sky had a frail blue quality in which the gulls seemed to float and bathe. But even the gulls could not be envied on a day like today because merely to sit on a shoreline boulder and let your hand touch the lapping water was gift enough.

So I rolled toward Duluth and Superior and took a medical inventory now and then of more than a thousand miles on the seat of a bicycle. There was very little sensation in my fingertips, and I blush to tell you I couldn't tie my shoelaces that morning or do all the zippers, including the crucial one. I was down about 10 pounds and found bruise splotches in the most novel places.

You wouldn't want to take a solo ride around Lake Superior every year. But in the aftermath I thought this: when you mingle all that sweat and excitement and tedium and discovery and have it coalesce in the sight of a great moose crashing into the woods at 5 a.m. as you alone confront it—that is the reward.

That and the thought that you and I, Andre, were brothers that day, and still are. The rubber held.

18

Kilimanjaro
Its Mysteries Unsolved,
Its Snowfields Vanishing,
But Still a Grail for Seekers

My dentist's office is normally outfitted with the usual time-killing defenses meant to insulate the clients from temptations to get impatient and surly: Here are month-old copies of *Newsweek*, *Vogue*, and *Sports Illustrated*, happy cartoons on the wall and a smiling receptionist.

I arrived for my semi-annual teeth-cleaning siege and unexpectedly found myself surrounded by photos of Kilimanjaro, the legendary mountain in Africa. The display was part of a montage, tastefully linked with photos of a climbing team that looked ready for an assault on the North Pole. One of the figures in the photos was my dentist, Dr. Phil Fabel, who now emerged from the hallway with a scrapbook instead of a scalpel.

I stared at the scrapbook, then back to the photos and finally into Fabel's triumphant eyes. "You've done it. You climbed Kilimanjaro."

Fabel acknowledged without further prompting that he had. He made a game stab at modesty, like you might if you

(Left) Layers of cloud give an ethereal quality to the historic Mt. Kilimanjaro in East Africa. Its summit snows are receding, but still not vanished.

won best of show at the state fair and gave credit to the fertilizer company. I'd been trying to entice him onto Kilimanjaro for years but his family and professional commitments kept intervening. The time came open for him in January of 2007, and with some of his biking friends he schemed a climb on the mountain.

Fabel is the kind of personality you encounter all too rarely, a professional man of relaxed social skills, easily motivated, instantly popular in any crowd and inquisitive about the world around him, whether on the bike path or in community theater, where I sometimes found him. Kilimanjaro was the one goal in his world of adventure. He wasn't a technical climber, but Kilimanjaro doesn't require technical experience. It is one of those instantly-magnetic icons of wild nature, rising to a height of 19,340 feet in equatorial Africa, above the rainforests, above the sweeping savannahs of the Africa plateau and above the remembered barbarism of the slave trade trail. It takes endurance to reach the top and, today, a fair amount of money. You can hardly blame the government of Tanzania for nicking those who come to climb Kilimanjaro. It's a stable country by today's standards in Africa, but still very poor.

I congratulated Phil seriously. He responded with a shrug and a grin intended to minimize his achievement. "You've done it five times, right?" he said.

I said, "My friend, you had this ambition of a lifetime. Kilimanjaro was a mountain you could climb, and it wasn't just any mountain. There IS something "beyond" about Kilimanjaro. And you sweated and grunted and worried about rockfall and you did it with people who had the same ambition, and you went to the top together."

It was a moment all of them would treasure, without boast or the need to explain. They would remember their fatigue and their gratitude and silent exaltation on top, standing on the summit together, without having to explain their goad to climb the mountain, if in fact they could. How did Hemingway describe the mountain he was later to escort into literature: "As wide as the world, great, high and unbelievably white in the sun."

Sometimes adventure for its own sake is completely acceptable and, incidentally, completely human. It doesn't have to be adorned with the rationalization of higher motive or humanitarian purpose. Most of the men

Between its summit crown and the great moors of its lower elevation, Kilimanjaro presents a moonscape that was actually used for training by the astronauts who landed on the moon.

and women who have gone into space probably were not drawn by the cause of advancing the interests of science or of country.

The thought of going into space was irresistible. No further justification was required.

George Mallory, who almost climbed Everest 30 years before the first successful ascent, once analyzed his motives this way: "Have we vanquished an enemy? None but ourselves. Have we gained success? The word means nothing here…We have achieved an ultimate satisfaction…A great mountain is always greater than we know; it has mysteries, surprises, hidden purposes; it holds always something in store for us."

Mallory loved to impute human qualities to the mountains. The impulse to do that with Kilimanjaro is almost impossible to avoid, as is the impulse to make it some kind of confessor to both the sins and the aspirations of humanity.

A few weeks before I first saw Kilimanjaro in the 1980s, a friend asked if I would listen for the bells when I reached the summit.

Some people who visit the remote or high places of the earth are touched by the notion or actual belief, invoked in these pages several times, in the circular movement of time. They suggest that the events of history and the struggles of people create echoes and vibrations that become a permanent part of time, sounding through the ages, moving in and out of history as though in mystical orbit.

Said my friend: These are the sounds you hear or think you hear if you are somewhere high in a strange land and in tune with the wind. Those sounds are like the bells of welcome, telling you that all's well in the world today.

It's a lovely thought and I said I would listen. With my friend Kjell Bergh, I climbed Kilimanjaro, led by an English-speaking Chagga tribesman and guide named William. His ancestors had been carried into slavery hundreds of years ago from the land spreading miles below us on the plains of Tanzania and Kenya. William lived on his wits as a promoter and trader in the Tanzanian village. But he also lived on his powerful legs as a mountain man and on his gusto as a saucy philosopher and singer of gospel songs.

He didn't spend much time interpreting Kilimanjaro for us. He assumed most people who come to his mountain know something of its history and spirit. It is one of the most gripping sights in the world because it stands enigmatic and isolated, rising from the rain forests and culminating in a vast dome from which the ice and snow have been receding alarmingly in the last few decades, perhaps some of the most dramatic evidence on earth of the price and destructiveness of global warming.

But in the year I first climbed Kilimanjaro, its crown was photogenic and draped in a huge snowfield. The mountain itself seems cast in the role of a historic presence, a kind witness to the ages, gifted with some secret wisdom. For the traveler who sees the clashing behaviors of nature as an allegory for those of humanity, a week on Kilimanjaro can be enticing beyond the achievement of a climb. It's as though the journey from a tropical plain to snowfield, from a relative paradise of the bougainvillea to the deep void of the dead but once-incendiary crater, might liberate us from the conflict we find both in the world and in ourselves.

But William made no plunges into metaphysics. As a guide, you'd give him high grades for ignoring sentimentality. It's an attitude which in the eyes of most guides seldom gets you to the top of a mountain. On Kilimanjaro William promised fatigue and nagging resentment over climbing in hours of freezing darkness in the early hours of summit day. He was an unabashed comedian. He also promised a summit sensation of utter relief. I told him this seemed to be a fair presentation of the mixed rewards of climbing. I asked how come he left out the fear of malaria and shell shock.

You can often climb on Kilimanjaro in the middle of the night without a lantern or flashlight. In the equatorial sky 3 or 4 miles above the sea, the moon and starlight radiating off the summit snow is (or was, in the years before the worst of the receding snows) enough. There are times when you feel you might be climbing on the moon itself. American astronauts had that sensation years ago when NASA brought them to Kilimanjaro's lava slopes above 15,000 feet on the Marangu route to condition them for walking on the lunar landscape. From that side of the mountain, still the one most commonly climbed, Kilimanjaro is fundamentally a trudge needing no technical equipment. Still it can be fascinating, the first three days on the route. It rises from the Tanzanian rainforest to 9,000 feet, into an otherworldly domain of giant lobelias and moors at 12,000 feet, and then on to the moonscapes at 15,000 feet. The last 4,000 feet to the summit ridge are disageeable, not unlike walking on a high-angle ash pile. But the final hour walk to the summit can shake out the fatigue and put you on an airy white ramp to the sun.

Even with the shrinkage of the summit snowfield, there are still moments when the climber can feel buoyed by the incandescence that far up in the sky, whether approached from the old standard route or the new one through more attractive terrain.

But on this, my first climb on Kilimanjaro, as well as subsequent ones, we adhered to the older protocols, and for two nights we slept in A-frames built by the Norwegians and then in the austere blockhouse at Kibo Point at 15,000 feet.

For the midnight breakfast at Kibo, William brought tea, biscuits and a couple of bananas. In 15 minutes we were moving upward on a rough trail through ash and shale and scree and in four hours we were on the summit ridge. We didn't need a rope. We did need long underwear, windpants and two wool sweaters because the windchill as we approached the summit was near zero. The sun's first pale orange streamers were dissolving the night. The climber was struck by the shifting synergies and collisions on the gigantic ceiling of the universe overhead, sunlight erasing the power of darkness, starlight blinking out, the snowfield defining the dominion of earth. The volcanic mountain, once explosive, now dormant, was at the center of this conflict of forces. Fire and ice, heaven and earth, illusion and reality.

William the guide and gospel singer took on a new role above the crater that bored into the mountain hundreds of feet below. He pointed to the place where the leopard carcass was found years ago. A plaque commemorates the bizarre finding. Ernest Hemingway used it as a riddle to begin his short story, "The Snows of Kilimanjaro." What was the leopard , an animal of prey, doing thousands of feet above its natural habitat, in an arctic environment where no prey lived? What are we doing, Hemingway seemed to be asking, trying to find meaning out of the unknowns and inscrutable parts of our lives?

William wasn't reflecting on these imponderables. He was singing. He gave us a chorus of rollicking hallelujahs when we got to the top and then shifted from the gospel to an African love song. He did a brief dance, not to appease ancient gods dwelling in the innards of Kilimanjaro, but in simple celebration. The sun was up. We were four miles in the sky. His clients discarded their fatigue and let their eyes roam the landscape. The world was still in repose in the early morning. For all of the grief that his people had known, William was able to sing.

The illusions and reality of that moment slowly disengaged. The illusion was that we have imparted something profound into our lives by climbing this mountain. What we had done was to unite our sweat and our imagination with an exotic part of the earth and reach a goal. The reality was more powerful. The reality was the great plain in the distance, the place where slave traders dragged thousands of human beings from their homes and their land. The mountain was the landmark to that inhumanity. But the mountain couldn't hear the cries for deliverance. It was stone and ice.

Yet on the morning we climbed to the top, the mountain did echo to the voice of William, a free man mirthfully singing his ballads. When we reached the summit ridge I remembered my friend asking whether I would hear the faint bells of moving time and humanity.

What I heard was the song of William, the free man. The bells and his songs may have been one and the same.

For all of its misery and bloodshed and poverty, Africa is irresistible to the traveler. It is mystery and glorious nature, forbidding nature, treacherous

For visitors to the great African plateau and savannah, the first sight of a giraffe is the coloring book of their childhood come to life.

nature; it is the stubborn dignity of men and women demeaned by poverty and obscurity, but not hammered down.

Some of the stereotypes need revision. Is there wholesale hunger and poverty here, corruption, AIDs, civil war and cruelty?

There is. But thousands and perhaps millions are looking to better lives today than a year ago, five years ago. There is a growing entrepreneurship in the more stable parts of Africa—Tanzania, Kenya, Uganda, Ghana and others. Representative government is getting some traction here and there. The great power of micro-finance, self-employment created with small loans that must be repaid with interest, is bringing financial service, trust and social development to hundreds of thousands. Those loans ARE being repaid at the incredible rate of 97 percent of the loans made by financial partners in the industrialized world.

The gift of traveling in Africa when you are liberated from synchronized time schedules is to discover personalities like William and Aadje Geertsema of Lake Ndutu. They lift you bodily into the novels and the testaments of the men and women who came to Africa when it first opened to the adventurers and poets. With them came save-the-animals idealists, the dreamers, the vagabond scamps, the evangelists, the daktaris with their medicines and their skills, and the humanitarians. Thank God for most of those. The imperialists who actually controlled Africa didn't make it especially easy for these people to navigate. But the romanticists and the healers made the industrial west pay attention. The Williams of Kilimanjaro belong with them because they became a bridge between the awful poverty of Africa, the violence of it and the exploitation of it, and the Africa of what is possible. Young people like William listened to the dreamers and the builders, went to their schools and began to make lives for themselves.

Aadje Geertsema became one of those builders, and now it is almost impossible for her to leave. Africa is her life and her grail but you're not likely to find her writing poetry. The lodge she manages at Lake Ndutu was once the haunt of big game hunters and the explorers of the awakening Africa of the early 20th Century. But the lodges need a practical head more than a troubadour.

Aadje came from Holland as a young woman intent on writing a paper on small wildcats for an academic degree. She met some of the European expatriates who were lodge keepers in Tanzania, and she settled at Ndutu. The last time I saw her, she was still a slender, attractive and wondrously competent woman, approaching her 60s, irreversibly a woman of Africa.

She would check the kitchen and greet the native bartender, and do the bookkeeping. But there were times when Aadje would sit by her fire beyond the lodge, on the edge of the posted wild country where big cats sometimes crept. She would look out on the alkaline lake, at the flamingo crowding together in the twilight, and her attitude suggested that she would simply rather be alone.

Her place, the Ndutu Lodge, had a special character unlike the expanding and luxury-appeasing big resorts that are beginning to dominate the wildlife observatories in Tanzania and Kenya. It offered comfort and clean and sturdily-appointed guest rooms, but there was still an aura of the African frontier there, and Aadje was the last person on earth who was going to change that special character. Ndutu is an East African crossroads on the edge of the Serengeti and west of the enormous Ngorongoro Crater, where thousands of animals live in a sunken wildlife sanctuary 18 miles across. Straight through Ndutu each year come a million honking wildebeest in migration. It was during one of those migrations that an animal later named Wildy wandered into Aadje's life and might someday become part of a child's coloring book.

Years ago a wildebeest calf emerged from the bush, about to die because its mother had been killed by hyenas. Aadje and her people gave it water and sent it back into the bush. They did the same when it reappeared for the next day, and the day after. But after two weeks of this, the little orphan failed to appear one morning.

"We thought the hyenas got it," Aadje said. They didn't. Aadje saw Wildy a few days later, munching grass with a herd of hartebeest, which look like a big deer. In contrast, the wildebeest resembles a sick cow.

"Wildy though it was a hartebeest, and we lost track of it," Aadje said. "Six months later, the wildebeest herd came back and up to the lodge walks this one. It had to be Wildy. It's been doing that for three years now, whenever the herd moves."

So right on schedule, Wildy strolled up to the lodge the week we were there, bringing 30 hooved friends with him. All of them got a shot of water from the drainage ditch. They scattered quickly, because the lions had the same idea.

Aadje Geertsema might have lived comfortably in her native Holland as an educator, photographer, clothes designer or rich wife. One visit to the great Serengeti Plain in the early 1970s dissolved any such temptations. She immersed herself in Africa. It was her marriage and her canvas. Her friends tend to be the Africans who work for her, plus that little colony of European entrepreneurs and adventure-seekers who have not completely vanished since Ernest Hemingway wrote about leopards and Kilimanjaro. Hugo van Lawik, an internationally renowned photographer, operated a camp a mile away and Hugo and Aadje had a beer together when the tourists got too thick or when the wildebeest charged north.

With apologies, I intruded at her campfire vigil one evening, exercising the modest privilege of a longtime visitor to Ndutu. I admired her not only for her allegiance to an idea and to another time but for her need to assert her privacy in a remote and harsh world that demanded some interdependence. We talked quite often, courtesy talk. Once in a while we talked about Aadje. She sat in jeans and wool sweater in front of her small wood fire, looking meditative. But she smiled an agreeable welcome and said something kind about my group and something she'd read in my accounts of travels in Africa.

"People ask if I get lonely," she said. "No, not really. Frustrated, yes, because this is a very poor country that is trying hard but doesn't have enough money to keep up its roads and build up its communications. We're stuck out here sometimes at the mercy of nature or simply our remoteness.

"But I don't want to leave. Margaret Kullander (an 'Out of Africa' type who is an institution in Tanzania) bought this place when it was running down in the 1980s. We've tried to preserve that character of it from another generation, when the visitors could feel intimate with the wild country but still feel comfortable. I think we've done that."

Her lodge was prospering on our last visit. The cottage amenities are modest and sometimes the plumbing has glitches and you couldn't get electricity from her generator before 6 p.m. or after 11 p.m. But the dining room was enchantingly open to the African air and sounds. Banana palms enfold the timbers of the ceiling. In the rafters now and then you can spot a small wildcat of the kind Aadje tracked from treehouses in the acacias for two years. In the end she wrote an academic paper that is still considered the most authoritative on small cats in Africa.

And the larger animals? And about danger?

"No, no, I don't fear the animals. Getting people to think clearly and reasonably in a crisis out here worries me more than being attacked by an animal. Mixing cement shouldn't be a crisis. But it can be if your place is 100 miles of bad road from the nearest city, and you're away from the lodge, and nobody has quite learned how to mix cement. I have 50 African men working for me. They're marvelous people, gentle and considerate for the most part. But they haven't taken any technical training to do some of the things that have to be done in a safari lodge. I didn't really get any training myself. You learn out of desperation.

"The first time I had to put in an order for a lorry (truck), I almost wet my pants. What did I know about lorries?" Today she drives them, repairs them and nurses them. She fixes Land Rovers and broken water tanks, the ones that store the rainwater, which is the only source of drinking water for her guests and employees. When the lodge needs new cottages or tent houses, she becomes an architect. If the resident pride of lions is short on drinking water, she runs a drainage ditch into the savannah and acacia groves on the other side of the clearing. She isn't sure what she's going to do about the buildings' foundations, because earthquakes and volcanic activity are occurring more frequently on the Serengeti and some of the tremors have cracked the concrete.

Not long before my last visit, she supervised the extraction of an elephant that got stuck in one of the water wells. In most business and callings in life, being foolish or disorganized will dump you into bankruptcy. In Aadje Geertsema's, it can get you killed.

Yet those who meet her instinctively envy her, they and the hundreds of others who have admired her tough intelligence and willingness to risk her life in the Africa that is now an inseparable part of both the woman she is and the light she follows.

I got up to leave, meaning goodbye for another year. She put her hand lightly on my arm and winked mischievously. "I'll know when it's time to go," she said.

It didn't look to be any time soon.

If ever.

20

A Dreamer I Hardly Knew, My Father

If he had lived in another time, my father might have been a sea captain or a flagman on a flight deck.

Though he was the son of immigrants, the sea seemed to be in his blood, and during his childhood years my father poured over geography books and imagined a life roaming the seas. But when he was just a teenager his destiny put him in an iron ore mine, struggling to support eight younger siblings.

Years after he was gone, I traveled to some of the faraway places that were threaded through the geography books of his childhood years when, as the son of immigrants, he imagined a life at sea.

If he felt cheated, no one ever heard him grieve, certainly not the brothers and sisters who became part of the rising middle class in America because of his sacrifice, and his two sons, who received the college education that was never available to him.

In his later years I'd invite my father and mother to spend a week in the mountains where I often climbed. He'd laugh and tell me: "That's your country, mountains. I hunt and fish here in Minnesota. Lakes and woods. That's where I live."

I offered to drive them around Lake Superior, but they preferred the short rides from their home in Ely on Minnesota's Iron Range to a place called Gooseberry Falls, and there's a story there and an important piece of my heart.

How much do we really know about the forces that shape our lives?

One of my newspaper readers once asked me why I kept returning to places like the Teton Mountains of Wyoming, to Yellowstone in winter and to the Himalayas of Nepal.

It wasn't hard to find reasons, but maybe I didn't understand then that the true architect of that life was an iron ore miner who fished on the ice in winter and hunted in the fall and lived in contentment with his wife and two sons and with his garden.

I think I can explain that in a few minutes.

For more than 35 years my professional home was the city room of a newspaper. That was gratifying but it was also a kind of cover. What I did whenever I could was to run with the wind, into the stratosphere, above the Arctic Circle, following the wolves on snowshoes on Isle Royale, and to explore a hundred other places. One offshoot of all that rambling was a role I have taken for nearly 30 years, as the resident denmother of a travel club whose members include professors, truck drivers, therapists, clothing salesmen, engineers and biking grandmothers.

They have been my accomplices on treks in the Himalayas and camera safaris in Africa. We have beachcombed on the island of Santorini in the Aegean. We have bargain-hunted in the jewelry shops of Cairo and wallowed in rainstorms on 500-mile bike rides.

All of them would qualify as trusted travelers although very few of them as bionic creatures. But they would concur in what I've adopted as the club mantra: Everyone Has an Everest.

This does not mean that they all aspire to climb Everest. In fact none has climbed Everest. Neither have I. What this little axiom means is that almost all of them, all of us, nurse a kind of ideal, an ultimate in life. It can be a mountain top, but for most it's not. It can be a day when we share an hour of profound serenity on the trail with a loved one; or a triumph in our professional careers; or the last payment on that 15-year student loan.

And yet the experience of the heights, a physical achievement that combines endurance with a powerful emotional commitment to reach a summit—is still one of the dramatic symbols of human striving.

And why is that?

At different stages of our lives, most of us have been gripped by an unguarded impulse or a secret yearning to follow a new star or walk a different path that can give us an identity we did not have before. It does not have to be a permanently different identity, rather just one more identity that might captivate or comfort us.

There is no way to predict where that star will lead. But it can be transforming. It can take us into a totally new dominion of discovery and sensation. For a few, if danger is involved, it can also be deadly. For almost all, it takes us on a journey into the unknown, sometimes physical and almost always psychological.

A young man who grew up on a sugar beet farm in the American midlands spends a few days in California with his college friends. They invite him to a day of sailing on the coast, his first experience on the ocean. He clumps into the boat and apologizes for his awkwardness. They sail again the next day, and he has time to feel the immensity of the ocean and the excitement of turning into the wind. He returns each year on whatever pretext seems plausible. It's still new but now exhilarating. Five years later he moves to the coast and buys a boat, The ocean, sailing, and his life are bonded for as long as he lives.

What was the allure?

Maybe it was the power and the moods of the sea that invited him to discover a part of himself he had never recognized, a need to feel the raw and uninhibited might of nature and to let it run through his veins, to join his curiosities and energies with the infinities and mystery of nature.

James Ramsey Ullman, who for years was a biographer of the mountaineering experience on the world stage, believed that human beings are never as human as they are when they are reaching for something beyond.

It can be argued. But we know that some of humanity's greatest achievements have been delivered by men and women who looked beyond, some of them absorbing ridicule, some of them, like Gandhi and Lincoln, dying because they were willing to risk and reach for something beyond.

Our own day-to-day ambitions hardly belong in that firmament. But it's also true that when we take what my late and great mountaineering friend

Lute Jerstad called "one step beyond," we sometimes open a completely new and electrifying world that lasts a lifetime. And that exploration may very well spring from some of our early grapplings to discover ourselves or, more generously, to discover another part of ourselves.

I'm not sure whether this next will be an affirmation or a confession: But now in a later time of my life I've found it makes sense to conduct some kind of harmless cross-examination. I can admit that in the earlier years the thrill in climbing consisted less in getting to the top than overcoming those fears of the unknown and finding novel ways to express my energies and expand my horizons. The idea of climbing a mountain, leaping out of a plane in a 3,000 foot free-fall, or riding a hot air balloon (all of which I confess doing) didn't spring from the glands of a born daredevil. I biked 1,100 miles around Lake Superior in seven days and ran a marathon after two days and ten miles of training—and later made a rather significant rediscovery of sanity.

There were more rewarding and less self-destructive ways to travel the open road and to tap into my curiosity about what was around the corner.

It didn't all have to be done today. The mountain was still going to be there tomorrow if it snowed and hailed today. I slimmed down and regained athletic condition. I grew stronger and became, with added years of experience, a reasonably good and prudent climber. The fear was gone, replaced by a working confidence in the technique of climbing. And suddenly climbing became an exhilaration. Gone was a nagging need to prove that I belonged in the fraternity. Climbing, in fact, became the means to a higher fulfillment. Climbing meant embracing a day with trusted friends on the rope. It meant, on the most glorious days, feeling stirred when my face touched the mountain's granite. There was an aroma to the rock, especially after a night of rain. It smelled of living things, tiny green colonies of lichen. But for the climber there was something even more tantalizing in it, a mustiness working itself into the nostrils, evoking the geological ages. The living rock meshed with the time of creation.

Sometimes while I belayed my partner on the rope as he followed, unclipping the carabiners as he moved upward and retrieving the pitons that secured the rope, I had to smile at how improbable all this was: allowing myself these small reveries on a mountain climb. Then I reminded myself: They had no place in the middle of a hard friction move on a perpendicular wall. Concentrate!

Well, all right. The guy coming up behind me was secure. But I knew that the aroma of the rock would linger with me after I was down from the mountain. It would rekindle a time to remember, like the smell of charcoal on the fingers hours after the campfire dies.

Remembering the smell of the rockdust would recreate for me a climbing pitch where I grappled for a hold so long my knees trembled and my fingers almost went limp. And then I would find a crease for my fingers, and slowly lift myself to a skinny ledge, and then cross over to another ledge, and the rest of the route to the top was wide open, the Burma Road.

And down in the valley the next day, the remembered aroma of the mountain's rock dust brought back an intimacy so vividly that suddenly it became the incense of the mountain. And later, on the descent on Mt. Moran with Monte Later and Herb Swedlund in the Grand Tetons, we practically had to perform the Australian crawl, swimming through fields of sunflowers eye-high. So we swam through the flowers and sang, and what had begun as a mountain climb became an impromptu nonsense chorus, mountain climbers with their hardware jingling on their belts, reverting unapologetically to songs of their childhood.

Why not? When we're kids, we climb trees. Why? It gets us off the ground, onto another plane, moving upward through the leaves and branches to discover something new. What was new? We could do it. It made us a little different, because not all kids want to climb trees. It doesn't mean they are less brave. It may simply mean that they don't have to prove that they can climb trees. Climbers who feel forced to explain their reasons for climbing usually run up against the stonewall of George Mallory's, "because it's there," an explanation that has acquired a kind of terse profundity but was probably a cavalier throw-away line after a couple of brandies. There is truth in it, of course, but for most people who climb, the impulse to do it mixes the spirit with the glands. Climbing tolerates ego and even demands it.

But most climbers will tell you that the enrichments that live and make it worthwhile are the ones that reach the senses. It is what climbing imparts to the spirit that gives it validity, more than the gratification of walking on top. If part of the excitement is freedom, it comes from asking the body and mind to reach into their deepest recesses to achieve a goal. It is also fraternity, the moral uniting of those who share the wonder and risk. It takes them to a remote and guarded world where, for a few borrowed hours, their blood and spirit can race with the wind and reach for the sun.

Most of my friends who climb rarely enter that debate. Like a few billion other people, I love life, cherish it and hope to advance myself at least well into another decade. This does not mean that I haven't relished the pure thrill of ascending a Matterhorn or a peak in the Himalayas. I have to admit owning a streak of the wanderer, and I've reached a pleasant conclusion that it might have been an inherited trait from my father, who did very little wandering at all but who was a dreamer still. He never saw the ocean he hoped to sail and never watched a sunset in the mountains.

He did manage one hair-raising ride on the rails in the middle of the Depression before settling into the predictable life of provider, miner, hunter, and gardener.

My father, Mike, worked for 35 years in an underground iron ore mine in the town of Ely on the Vermilion Range in northern Minnesota. His parents had died by the time he was 15, the oldest of nine children.

There were no welfare departments or social security checks when my father was a boy. The choices open to him were to arrange foster care for most of the children, or to keep the family together with income available from only one source—him. Splitting the family was not an option in those years. He had to find work. It meant ending his education in the eighth grade and closing the book on his private fairy tale— that he would some day sail on the high seas.

The few books visible in the family's small frame home near the iron mines were the sea epics Mike brought from school and the public libraries. In fact, there was an ocean of sorts not far from where he lived, the great freshwater sea of Lake Superior. He imagined life as a crewman on an ore boat or sailing the great oceans. On one of the walls at home was a painting of a schooner surging into the ocean waves.

The painting lit his imagination. He could finish school. He could get a high school diploma, and it would take him anywhere in the world. He would sail into the exotic ports he had memorized from the colored maps.

The mining towns of northern Minnesota in the early 1920s were rarely kind to the fantasies of a 10-year-old boy. Five years later he carried his lunch pail into the elevator the miners called "the cage," its walls reddened thick by ore dust. It lowered them 1,500 feet into the damp tunnels of the Zenith Mine, where the men, and at least one 15-year-old boy, began working 10 hours a day.

If my father ever looked on the underground mine as the dead-end of his boyhood visions, or saw himself as a captive of the cold-blooded economic system of the immigration years, he never mentioned it to me in the more than 40 years I knew him. I doubt that he felt that way.

What I do know is that somehow, in the mysterious passages by which the parent's yearnings and impulses are bequeathed to the child, the world of open seas and faraway places that was closed to him was thrown open to me.

It's one reason why I have stopped at least a hundred times over the years, when I drive the North Shore of Lake Superior, at Gooseberry Falls, which comes leaping out of the tanglewood of fir and birch and aspen flanking the Gooseberry River. It pours over the hematite cliffs in two leaps of a hundred feet of so, piling up blankets of foam that float on the root beer-colored pools beneath the falls.

The four of us visited Gooseberry Falls for the first time in 1936, my mother and father, my baby brother Dick, and I.

In all of my travels in the decades that followed, in the Himalayas, the Alps, on the Inca Trail, the great Rift Valley of Africa and dozens more of the earth's spectacles, I have never felt quite the same sensation of wonder or the strange benediction that came over me at my first sight of that waterfall.

I don't know whether it was my father's actual intent to open my eyes to another world, but that was the result. Our ultimate destination was the harbor in Duluth where my father made his annual pilgrimage to see the Coast Guard Cutter Woodrush. It represented the ideal of the sea life he never achieved. He didn't describe it that way, but after a few years we pretty much understood. In the subsequent years, Gooseberry Falls became a kind of medallion of my life in the outdoors. It was a revelation in my life and therefore was something to cherish. On each drive along Lake Superior's North Shore, for the next 50 years and more, I would park my car beside the highway, walk down the stone steps to the edge of the river and take a few minutes for thanksgiving. I still do that. Its the last place where he and my brother and I walked together, a few months before he died.

Conceding that moments like those leave absolutely no mark on the course of the universe, I still revere them as times when we can treasure the personal history we have lived. A family took a day to travel together in one of the darkest times of the country's economic life. I don't much linger today over the privations of that dark time. I do linger over that first sight of Gooseberry Falls. The innocence and wild beauty of that waterfall, romping in the sun, took hold of me that day in a way that lifted and stretched my horizons. Of all of the gifts I received from my mother and father, this one has outlasted almost all the rest. Who is to say what are the lasting influences that set us on the road we eventually take?

You won't find Gooseberry Falls in the geography books. It's dwarfed by the renowned cataracts of Victoria Falls, Iguaçu, the Yosemites and Niagara. But to a kid of 8 it was full of might and thunder. As I got older Gooseberry became a renewal and something of a marker in the passage through the seasons of my life, all of which stirred a genuine loyalty. But I drew something else from it the day of that first encounter with the waterfall, a feeling that lingered after the sound receded. I felt a warmth and composure walking down the trail with my father. And I realize now—without in any way attributing blame-- that it was one of the few times in our life together that I felt emotionally close to him.

So, a question. Can a waterfall evoke feelings beyond wonder and excitement? Maybe it can evoke regret; wistfulness about the might-have-beens. When I was a boy my father was the head of a household with responsibilities clearly formatted by the cultures and the boundaries of his times. My brother, Dick, was four years younger. Neither of us had any spectacular rap sheet of misbehavior; he rarely disciplined us and never struck us. He talked cordially when relatives and friends visited and at work he was a man admired by his peers. He supported us and tried to advance our interests both in and out of the classroom, rewarding us with his approval and sometimes with appropriate pin money here and there. Our environment was the mining town and most of the men worked underground. Many of them were immigrants from Europe or first generation stock. And although there were 25 bars in Ely, I don't remember any protracted hell-raising in town.

But it was hard for my father to extend demonstrative love to his children. It just wasn't done or deemed necessary or paternal in those years.

My mother nourished us and embraced us, ordered us to take piano lessons, made excuses for us when we copped out on the lawn mowing, and gave us the last ounce of care and love. In the rules and mores of the time, most men were not especially skilled in the arts and craft of frolicking with their kids; nor were they especially aware that this might have been a helpful line of behavior for both sides. Our childhood therefore was eminently normal. The regret I felt in later years, walking alone down the trail to Gooseberry Falls after he was gone, was simply not knowing this good and decent man better than I had. If there was fault, it was hardly confined to him. My parents lived all of their lives in northern Minnesota, Dick and I lived and worked 300 miles away in Minneapolis and Rochester. The fault when I was well into my adulthood may have been largely mine in not taking the lead more than I did, opening the door to some sensible common ground that would have created the social bonding that I never achieved. It matters to me now. And I admire the ease with which my brother Dick managed it. The two spent weeks hunting almost annually and Dick truly did discover a man neither of us knew as children. In the woods dad was amusing and thoughtful, a good listener and a companion who wore well, and rarely missed a target. I didn't hunt and didn't experience that kind of relaxed scrimmaging in the deer shacks and the card games.

But we weren't strangers. We took in three or four professional football and baseball games in Minneapolis and we enjoyed the man-to-man talk over a drink. In midsummer one year I flew up in a rented light plane and asked if he'd like an aerial view of the Superior National Forest, the part that was open to relatively low flight. He accepted quickly and I think what followed might have been one of the exhilarations of his life. He'd hunted and fished in that part of the world since he was a teen-age kid, and this was a sight of his lakes and woods from the air, a 200-square-mile panorama. His spontaneous delight was what we all felt when we saw the multicolored globe of our earth through the astronauts' cameras in space. I offered him an aerial map and told him he was officially designated the navigator of our Cessna 172.

We went through a 30-second briefing on orientation, and not unlike a train conductor, he began calling out the names of the lakes and rivers where he had fished. Swiveling in the passenger seat, he soaked up the great spread of green carpet below and the blue threads of the streams and the sprawling lakes. He didn't try to conceal his exuberance and after a half hour he had a proposal. "Would it be okay to fly a few miles into Canada?" I couldn't honestly tell him that it was but I doubted that the Canadian Air Force would send up attack jets for violating its air space with a Cessna. So we inched a few miles into Ontario and then came back flying over the Echo Trail. But now we were on the approach leg to land.

In those days the Ely airport had the stubby contours of a weed-infested sandlot. It also had power lines nearby and the town graveyard flanking the north-south runway. As we made our approach he asked me another question, trying not to sound worried. "Those runways," he said, "they don't look very long from up here." I agreed. "They don't look very long down there, either," I said. But we checked the windsock and came in low over the cemetery. Dad's shoulders looked a little hunched. I pulled up the nose about 100 yards from the end of the runway to cut the speed and landed in reasonable style.

He shook my hand and clapped me on the back. "That was something," he said. "I never thought I'd fly."

I don't know what took me so long to think of it.

But my father never spoke about the sacrifices in his life.

When, at 15, he walked into the office of the Pickands Mather Mining Company in Ely and asked for work, the supervisors were familiar with the death of his parents and the youngsters' struggles to stay together. Quietly ignoring the child labor laws that governed the land at the time, they gave the boy work and he remained an underground miner for all of his productive life. Eventually he became a foreman widely respected by his crew. If he resented his boyhood ambitions being crushed by a decision he couldn't avoid, my father made no complaint. He worked, hunted and fished, cared for his brothers and his sisters, married when he was 21, fathered two sons and, when he died, left enough savings to provide for his wife, Mary, until her death at 91.

His one adventure was a beaut. His yen for open spaces put him on a freight train in 1930 when he was 25, and it wasn't exactly a cushy ride. In fact it was illegal. Iron miners didn't have the cash for the train ride from Ely to Milwaukee in those worst of hard times in America. Hopping a freight train in the dead of night was one way to get there. It was hairy and it violated at least one federal law, two town ordinances and the vows of a half dozen railroad detectives.

But thousands of otherwise law-abiding American citizens traveled that way, and my father made it without a scratch from Ely to Milwaukee—which was worth several thank-Gods and a dozen beads on the rosary at my mother's next appearance in church. He also did it without detection, which was worth even more.

He didn't boast about it in the story-telling time on Saturday nights at our home. The provocation of the trip was the chance to spend a few days with his married sisters, all of whom had settled in Milwaukee. The thrill of it, though, crackled in every episode he remembered. It was the one and only pure adventure of my father's life. And his periodic reminiscences of it, usually after one or two beers, must have finally exorcised the lingering disappointment of the life at sea that never materialized.

I didn't miss a word of his narration. I pictured a young man timing his leap onto the ladder of a flatbed freight train, making his way into an empty boxcar, striking up a friendship with vagabonds from Seattle who had already come aboard. It was the danger they shared, a friendship lasting for two days, and the memories of the railroad detective who tried to tail them—but not very hard.

In the last ten years of his life, I visited in their home more often, and marveled at the versatility of his skills and his low-keyed but always precise work as an amateur cabinetmaker, gardener, electrician, hunter, and metalworker. He worked quietly and efficiently, with a kind of easy control and sociability. Even in his last months, when he was weakened and tired, he produced something almost every day. And the morning after he died, blooming in his house were a half-dozen immaculately tilled little boxes of marigolds and snapdragons sprouting on the kitchen counter where he had left them a few days before.

Miners don't have the same relationship with the earth as farmers. For the farmer it is his life and heritage. For the miner, the underground earth might be a bread winner or an antagonist, but it is no place for things that grow and nourish. Miners have to attack the earth. Which might explain my father's fondness for a different, life-giving kind of earth, and his gentleness with the flowers he raised by the hundreds.

We kissed him for the last time on a hospital bed in Duluth, where he was dying of leukemia. My mother must have remembered, as my brother and I did, the thousands of times they had done the same before his daily departure for the mine. It was a ceremony that, while sincere, never really enthralled him. To be honest, my mother required it. Without knowing much about the actuarial tables of underground mining, she decided that if fate should intercede, our last sights and sounds together as a family should at least be properly affectionate. And so my father once marched a quarter of a mile back into the house through five-foot snow drifts to kiss mother at 6 o'clock in the morning rather than suffer his wife's chill retribution 10 hours later.

In the mining towns' cauldron of nationalities and immigrant ambitions, the unchangeable chemistry was this: that the children and grandchildren should have opportunities to grow and achieve in places more refined and more generous than the plain frame cloisters of the mining company locations where they lived.

My mother and father and the others adopted that as creed. They would have been the last people on earth to see their lives as something more important, but they were the essence of the maturing of the land and people. Their lives had that quality, and that sacrifice. And it takes no artificial breast-beating or sentimentalism for us to recognize that now.

The vision of a life at sea had gone out of my father's life more than 50 years before. But when he died he was still within sight of the one sea, Lake Superior, his ocean, the one that he did know more durably than one he imagined as a boy. And it was not far from the waterfall that became the one imperishable bond between us, in his life and death.

21

Sometimes the Wildness of Nature Is an Invitation to the Child In Us

As evening approached I came down from the heights of the island, and I liked then to go and sit in some secluded spot by the lake; there the noise of the waves and the movement of the water, taking hold of my senses and driving all other agitation from my soul, would plunge me into delicious reverie in which night often stole upon me unawares.

—Rousseau

The kid had fallen behind his parents to take pictures and was trudging up the trail in the Alps, looking lost in his thoughts. His head bobbed under a New York Yankee baseball cap with its visor turned backwards. He seemed tired and ready for the cable car down.

But he stopped in curiosity when he saw me resting on a large boulder beside the trail. I had parked my backpack by the boulder with the ice axe lying on the pack.

The boy looked at my equipment and my knee-length cords and climbing boots. "Do you climb mountains?" he asked. He was 11 or 12, an average-sized kid wearing white athletic shoes, jeans and a denim shirt.

I said, "I try to climb once or twice a year. I live in Minnesota and I come here when I can because these are some of the most beautiful mountains in the world."

"Are there mountains in Minnesota?"

"We call them hills. They're not mountains but when you hike to the top you can usually see a lot of water because we have 12,000 lakes in Minnesota. Where are you from?"

"Colorado. We have mountains that are almost like these. How come you have so many lakes where you live?"

" Minnesota was covered by a huge glacier thousands of years ago and when it melted it left a lot of those lakes."

"Are you coming down or going up," the kid asked.

"Coming down. There was a big snowfall last night and nobody can climb today because the avalanche danger is very high."

The boy came closer and picked up the axe. He felt the steel alloy head of it, and the slightly curved adze that is used to cut steps into hard pack snow.

"Are you afraid when you climb?"

He smiled diplomatically, I assume trying to take pressure off the stranger.

I smiled the same way. "I think the thing I'm afraid of now is that I might not be able to get there, that some of the places may be too hard to handle."

The kid looked at me seriously for a moment. It wasn't the answer he expected. "Would that be bad?" he asked.

And now I laughed. "You know, I think you should catch up with your mom and dad, and tell them that I'm glad you asked that question. It gives me something to think about. The answer is no, it wouldn't be bad at all. It means that sometimes just being here means you win and the day is good. I think when you get older you'll feel that way."

He put the axe down and headed up the trail, turning to wave before he disappeared. I waved, and headed down.

What did I take from my aborted climb?

A wild snowstorm struck the mountain at night. The sun came out blazing in the morning but the eager invaders had to take their ice axes, turn and go down. The scene when we descended was glowing. It offered fresh snow on the slopes, scoops of it shining in the pines and spruces, the mountain lovely and elegant but too hazardous for climbing. So when we went down I thought I'd fall behind the ad hoc group I'd met in the overnight hut. It gave me a chance to enjoy the hike down at leisure, stopping for tea and strudel at one of the café overlooks, walking in the sun, talking to kids, explaining the axe, remembering a song. Was that so bad?

The song. "Things don't just happen, you have to make them happen..."

Where did that come from? Were the lyrics some kind of summons to a grab-life-by-the-horns search for the big payoffs in life?

Actually, no. The tune was popular then. I remembered singing it on a solitary bike ride in Minnesota, years ago when the lyrics seemed to harmonize with my attitudes about discovering the world around me. It came to something like this: Whether you're guided by impulse or some fixed ambition—a star of your creation—when the time seems right to go after it, do it with energy and do it seriously.

The star could be an idea, a place, probably faraway, or something that requires action. It doesn't have to be over the rainbow. It has to have meaning in your life, and you may want it to last a lifetime. If you can't do it alone, find people who share your idea. If you want or need to be a leader, be an informed leader. If you're going to share the journey with friends, be sure they're the right friends.

I'd found the right friends—Rod Wilson, Doug Kelley and John Peterson in Minneapolis, Monte Later in Idaho, Gottlieb Perren in Switzerland. Werner Burgener in Switzerland, and I want to tell you about Werner and the Eiger in a few minutes.

So I sang that song from time to time, and the tune and its idea developed a rhythm with the landscape and the towns and even the weather. For me there was a charm and something pure about biking the open road. There was nothing masked or marketed about it and for me it was full of invitation. The open road was the sun and the breeze, some rain, sometimes silence; or dogs barking distantly, somebody driving nails into a roof. The sound of the hammer broke the quiet of the morning, but it wasn't an intrusion, because the day was benign. What I was feeling was the countryside coming alive with its true and workaday rhythms. The sounds were close enough to remind me of the daily benevolence and demands of life but not too close to molest the peace of the morning. At 6 a.m. there was no one else on the road and I did a few harmless figure-eights before a car emerged around the curve ahead. I was on my way from Red Wing to Harris, a town 60 miles north of Minneapolis and St. Paul, my second day on a ride from the Minnesota-Iowa border to the Canadian border. I put up my tent in a public park near a little brook outside the town of Harris and walked to a small café for a pizza to go. When I got back to my campsite I settled in the tent to munch and read.

While I was washing I noticed a couple of kids throwing a softball in a little ballfield near a bend in the brook.

After 15 minutes I felt somebody rattling my tent. I opened the flap and one of the kids, about 7, was standing there with his glove.

"Can you come out to play?" the kid said.

Somewhere back in Ely, in the mists of childhood, I think I used that line on next-door mothers.

I said sure. We played for an hour. I hit grounders and then we played a game. I don't know what it was called but we kept score and we were about to finish when one of the moms came over. She gathered up the gear and thanked me and said, "That was very nice of you." Years later one of the kids introduced himself after a talk I made in Minneapolis. He was studying for his doctorate in college, thanked me for the fielding lesson and said what his mom remembered best about the incident was the next day, when she walked to the brook and saw that I'd cleaned up the tent site, spick and span.

Small town America. The longer I go into the high country, the woods or the lakes, I find myself simplifying the experience and reducing its ambiguities, at least while I'm there. This doesn't mean reverting to some innocent child's view of the world and life but finding a focus for the value and meaning of the experience. The chance encounters of it, like the park in Harris. If we find peace and comfort in it, or something in it that reaches deep into our spirit (or soul if you wish), why do we need to probe for something else, a rationale that complicates our simple appreciation of a day on the road. Sigurd Olson, the naturalist, often looked at it that way.

Embrace the gift you have received, he said.

The gifts that came to Sigurd Olson were not hard to understand, those he embraced when he was away from the speed and tumult.

"There were special places of deep silence." he wrote. "One was a camp on a small island above the pictured rocks on Crooked Lake, a rocky, glaciated point looking toward the north, a high cliff on one side balanced by a mass of dark timber on the other. Each night we sat there looking down the waterway, listening to the loons filling the darkening narrows with wild reverberating music. But it was when they stopped that the quiet descended, an all-pervading stillness that seemed to absorb all the sounds that had ever been. No one spoke. We sat there so removed from the rest of the world and with such a sense of complete remoteness that any sound would have been a sacrilege."

Yes, the silences and the remoteness. But then there is the robustness of nature, and the pealing sounds of nature that invite the action-seeker in us, and one of the later and marvelous sensations I experienced in the mountains was the pure exhilaration available when I skimmed away all of the grimness of "challenge" and risk.

I want you to meet Werner Burgener.

He was one of the generational climbing and skiing Burgeners of Grindelwald in Switzerland, who occupied much of the history of climbing in what was called The Golden Age of Mountaineering in Switzerland.

The photo galleries in Grindelwald, Zermatt and Meiringen in Switzerland and in Chamonix in the French Alps are full of pipe smoking, mustached and bearded guides, some of them Burgeners and some of them looking rather fierce. But this one was a Burgener of the late 20th Century, lithe, talkative and agreeable, with a museum guide's obsession to inform.

Climbing The Eiger in the Bernese Oberland was to mountaineering in the middle of the 20th Century what barrel-riding over Niagara Falls was to daredevils in North America in the 19th Century. It was never done very well and it was rarely done without burial rites afterward.

The Eiger constitutes the northern extremity of the alpine Oberland. Its north face or Nordwand has absorbed the ferocity of the north winds and ice storms for eons, creating a precipice more than a mile in height, a wild matrix of seamed rock, ice imbedded in the cracks around the calendar, overhangs, thin waterfalls and loose flakes.

Naturally, this combination eventually attracted climbers, some of them glory-seekers, some of them normal, all of them powerful climbers. They focused on the Eiger Nordwand when almost all of the other climbing problems had been overcome in the Alps. These included the Matterhorn's North Face, the Aiguille du Midi in the French Alps, and the rest. The Eiger had been climbed by its ridges but never the North Face until four German climbers did so in the 1930s. Others had died in earlier attempts and more would die after the first ascent. Better equipment and advanced technique inevitably made the North Face negotiable, if still hazardous, to new waves of climbers. For anyone who climbed in the 20th Century, the North Face of the Eiger remained an icon of the climbing-in-the-extreme cult. I'd looked up at the North Face during a half dozen hikes beneath it, and finally on a climb not on the North Face but the Mittelleggi Ridge, a long and classic skyline, the left ridge of the Eiger when seen from the resort town of Grindelwald in the valley.

Somebody recommended the name of Werner Burgener. I was moving well into middle age the year I called him, but I was in good physical trim and felt strong. We met at the railroad station in time to catch the Eisenbahn, a train that runs through the Eiger from Grindelwald after stopping at the alpine resort of Kleine Scheidegg beneath the Eiger mountain. The train then takes tourists into the heart of the mountain and from there to the Eismeer, the frozen lake lying among the mountain triumvirate of the Eiger (Ogre) the Monch (Monk) and the loveliest of the three, the Jungfrau (Young Woman). We were going to ride half way and begin the climb from a trail that joins the Mittelleggi.

Werner Burgener was sociable, effervescent, and basically hard to resist. He said we were going to have a great climb on the Mittelleggi and we were going to enjoy it, and I could forget all about the ghosts of the North Face and its fearsome reputation. "We're climbing the Mittelleggi not the Nordwand," he said. "It's a long and beautiful ridge. You have to be a good climber to do it but it gives you an Eiger experience you will never forget. And wait until you get to the descent!"

I said I would be content first to get on the Eisenbahn. We got off at the station near the trail to the overnight hut and began making our way to the ridge. At first exposure it didn't look or sound like a happy-days frolic. Avalanches crashed around us every three or four minutes. Blocks of ice as big as hotels broke away from hanging glaciers and fell in clouds of exploding crystal. It was a gallery of primeval bedlam and it was stunning.

"Some performance," Werner said. He was mischievous. It was his milieu and he was energized by it.

Some mountain, I said. It wasn't my normal habitat but I couldn't resist it. When you shake out most of the rhetoric, the urge to climb usually sifts down to two things: the normal curiosity to find out what's around the corner; and the fuel of adrenaline that you bring to an action that can't be successful without some level of risk. But if you have any sense you also recognize the one side of risk that makes it acceptable: It ought to be manageable. Wild and hairy risk will get you killed. We weren't getting into that soup today. My approach to minimizing the risk was to tie into a man who knew the mountain. This was not going to guarantee safety but it was going to be the difference between watching those ice blocks roll down the mountain 500 yards away and being squashed by them. Once you have dealt with the psychology of danger you can tend to the brass tacks of trying to get up the mountain. You can also enjoy it if you understand your capabilities and limits. Sometimes, when your body feels strong and the sun is warm and the company is good, climbing high-angle snow and rock can be a romp. The mental exercise in successful climbing is basically the same as it is for successful painting or juggling. It is one move at a time, and only the foolish relaxes his concentration to ponder the grand design of it. I can't think of anybody silly enough to relax on the Eiger.

The first climbing rock we encountered was loose and lousy limestone. The angle of ascent below the Mittelleggi hut wasn't severe, so it didn't' matter much. Handholds that looked as secure as Fort Knox flaked in your hand. You couldn't trust the rock and you couldn't trust the ice, which made it a suitable introduction to the Eiger . We got to the overnight hut in two hours. To relieve the unsettling cannonade of avalanches and rockslide, the sky offered diversity. It started to hail. The stones weren't big but compensated by being mean. After 10 minutes of it, we made it inside the hut, had some boiled sausages for dinner, slept for seven hours, had breakfast of boiled sausages and at 5 a.m. roped up and started the ascent of the Mittel-leggi before the sun.

The ridge was thin but the sky was clear and the loose rock disappeared, giving way to firm limestone and gneiss. With each step the angle steepened and with each step came the reality that this was no ordinary mountain.

Nearly 7,000 feet below, the lights of Grindelwald blinked. Under our boots the massive ice field of the Eiger's slope fell away into the vacuum. I felt good about our partnership. Werner stopped taking his methodical delays at the fixed protection points, where he would make sure he was clipped in to the belay stake and had a good stance. After a while we began climbing in uninterrupted rhythm. By mid-morning it was a song. We were both fit and moving. The rock pitch we were on lifted almost to the vertical to reveal great lengths of fixed ropes intended for both safety and speed. Sometimes we needed them, sometimes not. We were practically flying and it was glorious. Snowfields crunched beneath us, then rock. It went for two hours that way. Then some towers of snow and ice that we could outflank. Ahead we could see the great white coxcomb of the Eiger's summit.

Werner now chose to reveal a mania for the museum guide's precision. At the top of each rope length, while I busied myself discreetly sucking in the thinning air at 13,000 feet, Werner insisted I should have perspective. "Here we have an even better look at the surrounding peaks of the Berner Oberland," he said. "There is the Wetterhorn and swing around to the Schreckhorn and the Finsteraarhorn and, wait a minute, migawd, you can see the Weissmies way out there to the southwest, and that huge clump of white is Mt. Blanc. Don't you think this is tremendous?"

I said only a lout would fail to see that it was tremendous.

"Mt. Blanc, that floors me," he said. "Can you believe it?" I told Werner I was a man of unshakable faith. If Werner identified the white clump as Mt. Blanc, I would carry that knowledge into hell. Werner's eager orientation actually unhinged me for a while. You put on a game face before a climb like this and I had stirred my juices right up to the red line, where it reads "combat-ready." This mountain had that kind of reputation. And it's true that if you're not careful the climb can get top-heavy with melodrama, a caricature of war, and there I stopped myself.

The highly-motivated amateur can get caught in the theatrics of going to the top and damn the odds. The folly of it was summarized decades ago by an old guide's terse reply to an English climber who shouted out in excitement when he thought he saw a route to the summit that was actually highly dangerous.

"*Es geht,*" he yelled up to the guide, meaning "it goes."

"*Ja,*" the guide responded, "*Es geht, aber Ich gehe nicht.*"

It goes, but I don't.

Here on the Mittelleggi we had no divided opinions. We were going. We were going to the top together and reveling in it. Werner jabbered. His face was animated and aroused and it extended immediate comradeship. He was a jewel for a companion, and he never bothered with the postures of his trade.

The fixed ropes on the steepest section opened the way to the summit. "Your technique is good," he said. "Are you ready for another history lesson?"

When we reach the top, yes, I said. But the long snow crest was narrow and icy. The snow on the south side was more compliant. It also was more seductive. It was an insurance seller's nightmare because sections of it were supported by nothing but 5,000 feet of thin air. The climber calls it exactly what the architect calls it, a cornice.

We stayed right or north and hurried over the thin track toward the top, looking down the long shadowy throat of the Eiger's North Face. Down there were old fixed ropes, testifying to the history of the Eiger Nordwand, the frozen bodies that had dangled there for months before being cut down, but also the belay stakes near the summit that marked the successes.

But this wasn't war. The sun was here overhead, filling the snowfields and the summit crest with diamonds. And now we were on top, together, alone in the sky. Werner shook my hand, we clasped arms and waved to the Grindelwalders two miles below. Then we walked down the south slope a few yards and snacked.

"Going down we could go the easy way, by the opposite ridge," Werner was saying, "but you're going very well and I'm going to give you the greatest descent tour on the Eiger." I gulped silently, trying to tell Werner, "thanks, but you don't put yourself to any trouble."

But he DID take the trouble, and we were off, and Werner was some kind of high altitude Jules Verne. He took us down four rock pinnacles averaging 750 feet high and then down a glacier beneath the Monch. Vast snow bowls opened up beneath us and it was sensational. I was tiring but it was still sensational. We crossed small snow bridges suspended a thousand feet in the air. We scampered up and down limestone steeples, front-pointing with two points of our crampons in spirals in the rock. It was a climber's vision of Oz. The route led up a rock chimney. At the end of it the sky erupted blue, as though a tunnel had been lifted to the vertical. We crawled through what the American Indians might have called a hole in the day. It was a wonder. The whole climb down was fatigue, spectacular sight lines, the Monch, the Eiger and the Jungfrau lifting their crowns above us, and streams of falling snow ignited by sunlight, dislodged by our movements. And then the streamers below us broadened and thousands of pounds of snow fell away from one corner of the ridge we were standing on, onto a glacier a half mile straight down.

The sight straightened my hair because we were standing just 18 inches off the fracture line when the snow let go. "I saw the line," Werner said. "We were safe." You can't be too careful." I offered no dispute. The descent had been almost literally out of this world, the most exciting and ultimately joyful hours I'd ever spent in the mountains. Nearing the long snow ramp that would take us to the Jungfrau station and the train that would return me to Grindelwald, Werner belayed from above while I walked backwards on the rope, my crampons digging in to the mixed snow and rock of the mountain wall, 50 feet down to the glacier. Werner fixed his own belay and came bouncing down in 15 foot leaps.

We walked up to the station. He grabbed my shoulders and looked into my face before we got there. "Tell me the truth," he said. "Was this a great day for you?"

It seemed important to him. It was a simple and touching attempt by a young mountaineer to mingle his spirit with that of his companion, and to find out if we were truly kin on the mountain.

I said: "Werner, I couldn't imagine a better day in the mountains." We shook hands for the last time, and he headed for one of the climber's huts where he would spend the night. The train was late, and I had time to lie down on one of the benches. Sometimes exhaustion can be luxurious, and it ought to be stretched out.

If this was to be a last climb on a major mountain, I'd be content today. It didn't have to be and it was not undertaken with that assumption at all. Old newspaper folk, who have been subjected to demonic indignities at the hands and the blue pencils of editors during most of their active lives, are chronically resilient.

But this was a day when my cup filled, and on the train to Grindelwald I actually offered a prayer of thanks.

A prayer. Why not that? I gave thanks for the unpredictable grace that moves in our lives, including the grace of an unforgettable day on a mountain. It was a day of romping in the snow achieving something worthwhile. What I was expressing was simply the joy of being alive in this tick of time.

It wasn't the day of serenity that flowed from Sig Olson's silences in the wilderness, or of someone else's pure humility watching the sunset over the Serengeti Plain in Africa. But it was drawn from the same springs of gratitude.

Can we return to those same springs on another day or years from now, and do it with the same reward?

I don't see why not.

People will tell us "you can't go back again," to that moment in the sunset in Africa or to the moment in the Khumbu of the Himalayas when you turn a corner of the trail, and the mountains, Ama Dablam, Themserku and the rest soar incandescent into the morning sky.

Yes, you can go back, because the part of you that you left in the Himalayan valley is still there, and that part is your yearning for something that you may have found, and need or want to renew.

What you found there is the spiritual quality of that moment, that day, or in that feeling of transformation.

The transformation doesn't mean out of body. It does mean something has changed in your life, that in one way or another the experience has become a part of your life and probably a part of your life when you felt the presence of something higher? And if not that, a reconciliation? A reconciliation with whom, or what?

Nearly ten years ago I wrote a book called *Pursued By Grace*, in which I told of my recovery from alcoholism and with it a kind of spiritual awakening.

I said: "I am among the least qualified candidates on earth to recommend which is the best road to personal peace. We live in a time when the information highway and the stresses of today's life have lifted the hunger for spirituality to the force of mania. It is, in fact, approaching a cascade in today's outpour of fixes for tense psyches and nerves."

Should we rejoice in this popular surge to discover the true key to spirituality?

Moderately might be a good way to rejoice.

Spirituality is a perfectly good word. It connotes depth of feeling that fosters serenity in us. It is a quality of being in contact with God, with a higher power or however the person who experiences spirituality chooses to define this force that puts one's life into a sphere of well-being. For some people spirituality has nothing to do with God. They seek a harmony with life in this and only this world. Which means an atheist can rightly claim to have achieved spirituality. Most of us will see in it—or try to—something divine.

But let's say spirituality is peace. That is simple and recognizable. It is what I want and what took me an enormously long time and years of self-indulgence before I could honestly approach it. The problem overtaking spirituality today is that the idea is so good and attractive that it has been commandeered by the get-well-this-instant industry.

As "The Answer" in our lives, it is being merchandised relentlessly. You can get spirituality in books, tapes, videos, and séances. This is good, old bottom-line capitalism. Identify a market. Serve it and hustle it. It's roughly the same treatment directed, at other healthy concepts like "intimacy" and "openness," marketing that produced millions of dollars in profit by convincing hordes of people that their lives were barren unless they knew the secrets of intimacy and openness. We were invited to work them over in all of our idle moments the way we worked on Rubik's Cube. Intimacy was defined, redefined, dissected and enshrined. It achieved the highest threshold of the get-well vending by being packaged into working manuals.

Spirituality is too important to be accorded this fate. A traveler on a tour with me a few years ago confided that he found his spirituality while staring at a flight of geese. I had no doubt of his sincerity. I did ask in what direction the geese were flying. He smiled at that but we did understand after the shared laughs that if we find spirituality in nature, we do not or should not draw boundary lines.

I think most of us who find nature an indispensable part of our lives and our destiny understand this. Nature and your God, if you have one, are not one and the same, but are part of one grace, the grace that moves in our lives and is available to us if we seek or simply if we understand. Nature is not bad because it erupts or floods. It does that in response to *laws* of nature. And where did the laws of nature arise? Or what is the source of that grace? Most of us aren't theologians. We can leave that to the reverends. But we know the beauty and peace we find in nature, whether we find it in our introspective moments during a walk in the woods or on the final rappel from a mountainside.

Or in the sight of canoers crossing a windy lake.

"I watched a couple of canoes beating their way across the open reaches of the lake," Sig Olson wrote. "The boys in them were singing and I caught snatches of their song. Stripped to the waist, they were using their strength to keep the slender craft from getting out of line in a high wind. Traveling by primitive means, I knew within them the long inheritance of a nomadic ancestry was surging through their bodies, bringing back the joy of movement and travel, adrenaline pouring into their veins, giving courage to muscles being strained to the utmost. If I had been close enough, I might have heard the laughter in their song, seen the glad light in their eyes. They were at home, doing what men had done for uncounted centuries…."

And what is that feeling?

"During the day you are part of the waves, judging them, coasting down the long slopes between them, only to climb to the top of another, and then do it over again, until you are completely drained of energy. Somehow the mind is washed clean, and when it is over the cleanness continues until you crawl into your sleeping bag for hours of dreamless sleep."

The nature that feeds us and cleanses us and unchains our spirits is the nature that brings us closer to the god in our lives, however we choose to define that god.

Namaste, they will tell you in the Himalaya. "I praise the god who lives within you."

We draw our replenishment from the woods and water, the mountains and the savannah. Can we go back again, to what seem the most precious times to us?

I think we can and, in fact should if it makes sense to us. For me an experience like the ones with Gottlieb, or Rod and Werner, or my friends in the Himalaya, cannot be placed in the gilded glass cabinet, a museum.

So, yes, we can renew a time and a sensation. When that is no longer possible, it can be replaced. Sometimes there is not that much difference between a walk on the Inca Trail and a walk through an arboretum.

What matters finally are the relationships that our unions with nature have fostered and enriched.

These can be renewed. It is not possible that they can be forgotten.

How can we possibly forget a word like "namaste?"